IN PURSUIT OF GOD

In Pursuit of God

The Life of A.W. Tozer

James L. Snyder

CHRISTIAN PUBLICATIONS
Camp Hill, Pennsylvania

Christian Publications
3825 Hartzdale Drive, Camp Hill, PA 17011

The mark of ✝ *vibrant faith*

ISBN: 0-87509-457-0
LOC Catalog Card Number: 91-71411

Printed in the United States of America

91 92 92 94 95 5 4 3 2

CONTENTS

Foreword 1

1 *Just Tozer* 3

2 *To Be Born Right* 11

3 *The Tozertown Farm* 17

Personal Glimpses: Childhood 29

4 *The Pursuit Begins* 33

5 *Tozer Begins to Preach* 49

6 *Indianapolis—Apprenticeship in Earnest* 63

7 *A Reluctant Candidate* 73

Personal Glimpses: The Personal Side 81

8 *Chicago* 89

9 *Preacher* 103

10 *Writer* 119

Personal Glimpses: Advice 131

11 *Editor* 133

12 *A Man of Prayer* 143

Personal Glimpses: Preaching 153

13 *Mystic and Prophet* 155

14 *Poetry and the Poets* 165

15 *Family Man* 179

Personal Glimpses: Council 197

16 *Potpourri* 201

17 *Toronto* 213

Personal Glimpses: Effective Ministry 223

18 *The Goal* 225

Appendix 231

Bibliography 235

Foreword

I am often asked, "Was Dr. Tozer the greatest preacher you ever heard?" No, but he redeemed the time and hence had an intimacy with God beyond any other man I ever met. He was a modern mystic who had given priority to the lost art of meditation. To enter into Dr. Tozer's presence was an awe-inspiring event.

He was not just a prominent author, he was an eminent one. His writings still reflect the "anointed ability to speak to the present need of men's hearts." He could articulate wisdom in an amazing economy of words. On one occasion he said to me:

"I have to account to God not only for what I have done, but for why I did it."

His most memorable words to me:

"There are occasions when for hours I lay prostrate before God without saying a word of prayer or a word of praise—I just gaze on Him and worship."

I advise every Bible student with whom I have contact by phone or by letter or in person: Buy all the books Dr. A.W. Tozer has written and digest them.

To know Dr. Tozer was a great blessing. To pray with him was to be in the Holy Place! wow

Leonard Ravenhill

"I consider Dr. Tozer the most remarkable man of God that I have known personally. In my opinion, his greatest gifts were prophetic insight regarding biblical truth and the nature and state of the evangelical church of his generation. He was respected highly even by those that considered him severe and aloof but to those who knew him, he was gracious and kind. I believe he was a lonely man, as many great men of God have been."

William F. Bryan
Minister, The Christian and
Missionary Alliance

1

Just Tozer

Fortunate is the person who, when going through a dry period spiritually, has a Tozer book at hand. The commentator who made that observation may have had in mind *The Pursuit of God* or *The Knowledge of the Holy*, A.W. Tozer's acknowledged spiritual classics. Or he may have been thinking of any one of the nearly 40 other books either written by Tozer or created posthumously from his recorded messages. Although A.W. Tozer died in 1963, his spiritual legacy continues to satiate those thirsty for the deep things of God.

Many familiar with the writings of A.W. Tozer know little about the man behind the books. Even during his lifetime most respected him but few understood him. By disposition and design, he walked alone, preferring God's fellowship to people's. His relentless pursuit of God—though not without price—accounted for his spiritual strength and resulted in the sustained popularity of his books.

Aiden Wilson Tozer was born April 21, 1897, in La Jose (now Newburg), a tiny farming community in the hills of western Pennsylvania. His mother named him for the storekeeper husband of a close friend from girlhood. He did not like his given names, preferring the initials, "A.W." In later life he preferred just Tozer.

In 1919, five years after his conversion, and without formal theological training, Tozer began 44 years of ministry with The Christian and Missionary Alliance. For 31 of those years he gained prominence as pastor of Southside Alliance Church in Chicago, serving there from 1928 to 1959. He ministered as a pastor, author, editor, Bible conference speaker, denominational leader and, was to many, a reliable spiritual mentor.

Many regarded him, even during his lifetime, as a 20th-century prophet. Discerning that modern Christianity was sailing through dense fog, he pointed out the rocks on which it could flounder if it continued its course. When other voices were but empty echoes, his proved to be the voice of God. His spiritual intuition enabled him to scent error, name it for what it was and reject it—all in one decisive act. He could tear to pieces in a few short sentences the faulty arguments of others.

Whether writing or speaking, Tozer always ministered to those hungry for God. He majored on the issues of paramount spiritual importance avoiding religious nonsense and trivia. People went away from his ministry with the haunting sense of just having been in the immediate presence of God.

Looming large in Tozer's public ministry was his editorship of *The Alliance Weekly,* the official publication of The Christian and Missionary Alliance. In 1958, *The Alliance Weekly* became *The Alliance Witness,* which in turn became *Alliance Life* in 1987. Under Tozer's leadership, the magazine's circulation doubled. *Alliance Life,* more than any one thing, established Tozer as a spokesman for the Alliance and to the evangelical church at large.

As a man prays

Tozer's real strength came from his prayer life. He often commented, "As a man prays, so is he." His entire ministry of preaching and writing flowed out of fervent prayer. What he discovered in prayer soon found expression in sermons, articles, editorials and finally in books.

A lively imagination and eloquent descriptive powers gave force and vividness to what Tozer said.

He spent hours meticulously preparing sermons that were majestic and profound. He learned to use crisp, precise, climactic sentences. He did not have a strong voice, but his message penetrated the soul. People never forgot what he said.

The discriminating care with which he wrote his books established Tozer as a classic devotional writer. Diligent labor paid off in a style and strength of expression that continually attracted readers.

During the mature years, 1951–1959, WMBI—the Moody Bible Institute radio station in Chicago—broadcast a weekly program, "Talks From a Pastor's Study," originating in Tozer's study at Southside Alliance. As a result, Tozer frequently received invitations to speak at Chicago-area Bible colleges, a ministry of special delight to him.

Throughout his ministry, Tozer issued a persistent call for evangelicals to return to the authentic, biblical positions that characterized the church when it was most faithful to Christ and His Word. Whether analyzing a text or explaining a Bible truth, he always sought to help listeners make the necessary decisions in their spiritual pilgrimages.

A major concern of Tozer's was the lack of spirituality among professing Christians of his day. He zeroed in on its primary cause. "I am convinced," he wrote, "that the dearth of great saints in this day . . . is due at least in part to our unwillingness to give sufficient time to the cultivation of the knowledge of God." Speaking about the frenzied pace set by religious leaders leaving no room for unhurried reflection and meditation, he cautioned, "Our religious activities should be ordered in such a way as to leave plenty of time for the cultivation of the fruits of solitude and silence."

While his messages were profound and sober, Tozer's keen sense of humor added a clever, yet sharp, touch. Contemporaries likened his humor to Will Rogers' honest homespun wit. Frequently it harked back to the Pennsylvania farm of his youth. Not a storyteller, he used the turn of a phrase, a grotesque simile or a satirical observation to get his point across effectively. Much of his humor was audience-dependent for its effect. Therefore, those who read Tozer will find little of it in his books.

Practice the presence of God

In daily life Tozer's sense of God enveloped him in reverence and adoration. His preoccupation was to practice the presence of God—to borrow a phrase popularized by mystic Brother Lawrence whom Tozer delighted to read. Reflecting on his relationship with God, Tozer once wrote, "I have found God to be cordial and generous and in every way easy to live with." To him, the love and grace of Jesus Christ were a recurring astonishment.

It is not possible to understand Tozer's life and ministry apart from his pursuit of God. "Labor that does not spring out of worship," he once wrote, "is futile and can only be wood, hay and stubble in the day that shall try every man's work."

Tozer's carefully hammered out convictions about worship dominated everything about him and his ministry. "Worship," he wrote, "is to feel in your heart and express in some appropriate manner a humbling but delightful sense of admiring awe, astonished wonder and overpowering love in the presence of that most ancient Mystery, that Majesty which philosophers call the First Cause but which we call Our Father in Heaven." This gave impetus to his entire life.

Tozer's hunger for God led him to study the Christian mystics. Their knowledge of God and absorbing love for Him profoundly attracted Tozer. They were spirits kindred to his own. "These people know God," he would say, "and I want to know what they know about God and how they came to know it." He so identified with their struggles and triumphs that people began referring to him, also, as a mystic, a designation to which he never objected.

Tozer's list of these "friends of God" grew with the years, and nothing delighted him more than to uncover a long forgotten devotional writer. He eagerly introduced these newly discovered mystics to his friends, bringing many of them into public awareness.

Not a perfect man, Tozer had his warts. A reclusive disposition, coupled with the demands of a too-heavy schedule, left little time for his wife, Ada, and his family. As a pastor he had little time or inclination for the individual nurture of his people, relegating those matters to others. Never deliberately nasty or venomous, he occasionally had to apologize to someone he hurt when he popped their balloons of pretense and pomposity.

Tozer remained faithful to His Lord to the very end.

Toward the end of his ministry he enlisted his church's prayers for a personal struggle. "Pray for me," he requested, "in the light of the pressures of our times. Pray that I will be willing to let my Christian experience and Christian standards cost me something right down to the last gasp!"

TOZER-GRAMS

I like a pipe organ in a church, especially where the preacher is a modernist. I enjoy counting the pipes and trying to guess which palm the console is hidden behind while the preacher distills his learned doubts over the congregation.

Samuel Boggs, late head of the Gideons, was a great lay preacher. He used to preach a thought-provoking sermon called, "Unknown Disciples." What a glorious company they were, those heroes and heroines of the Bible, whose deeds were recorded but whose names were not given!

There is another book kept by the One who never slumbers nor forgets, and in that book the anonymous great have their names as well as their deeds recorded. After all, a deed without a name is better than a name without a deed.

It is a dangerous and costly practice to consult men every time we reach a dark spot in the Scriptures. We do not overlook the importance of the gift of teaching to the Church, but we do warn against the habit of taking by blind faith the opinions of men—even good men. A few minutes of earnest prayer will often give more light than hours of reading the commentaries. The best rule is: Go to God first about the meaning of any text. Then consult the teachers. They may have found a grain of wheat you had overlooked.

PRAYER

Lord, I would trust Thee completely; I would be altogether Thine; I would exalt Thee above all. I desire that I may feel no sense of possessing anything outside of Thee. I want constantly to be aware of Thy overshadowing Presence and to hear Thy speaking Voice. I long to live in restful sincerity of heart. I want to live so fully in the Spirit that all my thoughts may be as sweet incense ascending to Thee and every act of my life may be an act of worship. Therefore I pray in the words of Thy great servant of old, "I beseech Thee so for to cleanse the intent of mine heart with the unspeakable gift of Thy grace, that I may perfectly love Thee and worthily praise Thee." And all this I confidently believe Thou wilt grant me through the merits of Jesus Christ Thy Son. Amen.

"The Sacrament of Living"
The Pursuit of God

"He keenly felt that the transmission of the spiritual heritage granted to the Church in trust for the world was in danger due to the inroads of religious sham and worldliness. His, therefore, was a clarion call for evangelicals to return to those authentic, biblical, personal and inward positions that have characterized the Christian Church when she was most faithful to Christ and to His Word."

Dr. Louis L. King
A.W. Tozer: An Anthology

2

To Be Born Right

Whenever someone asked Robert A. Jaffray, pioneer missionary to China and southeast Asia, what makes a great missionary, he would promptly reply, "To be born right the first time!"

Tozer delighted in that quotation because he was convinced of its truth. Parents and grandparents play a large role in shaping the lives of their progeny. Certainly many of Tozer's personality traits were the heritage of his English grandfather, Gilbert Snyder Tozer—a grandfather he never knew.

Gilbert Tozer began life in England in the year 1810. His surname came indirectly from the Scottish "thistle," a rough tool used for carding or "teasing" wool felt. Because a dog had sharp teeth, it also was called a teaser—or a towser. By modification this became the name Tozer.

A.W. Tozer would much later comment, tongue in cheek, that it was humbling to learn this bit of intelligence. But, apart from the grace of God, Tozer once remarked, he was only a thistle.

While still a boy, Gilbert Tozer followed the lead of many of his contemporaries and emigrated to the United States. He settled in upper New York State and before long married. When his young wife died, Gilbert moved southwest to Clearfield County in Pennsylvania. There he met Margaret Weaver, a girl from Westmoreland County. The two were married in 1850.

Together they built the first house in what is now Newburg. At the time, however, the locale became known as Tozertown, in honor of Gilbert. The marriage ultimately produced eight children—four boys and four girls.

Like many other local citizens, Gilbert soon established himself as a lumberman and a raftsman. In the winter he harvested and dressed the region's natural timber. Each spring he floated the logs down the west branch of the Susquehanna River in huge rafts, selling them to the various lumber mills along the route.

As Tozertown grew, Gilbert became concerned

about the welfare of his children. Not wanting them to grow up in a town environment, he believed a farm was the proper place to raise a family, especially if there were boys. So Gilbert bought a farm just outside town and moved his family to it. He himself continued to live in town, going to the farm only on the weekends—the boys cared for the chores. Gilbert did not expect much financial gain from the farm; his objective was simply to keep his boys out of trouble.

Gentleman farmer

On his weekend visits, Gilbert would bring a stack of newspapers, magazines and books to the farm. It was not unusual for him to spend the entire weekend reading. Neighbors nicknamed Gilbert the Gentleman Farmer. But what the neighbors thought or said did not bother him. He was doing what he believed to be right for his family, and nothing else mattered.

Just how religious Gilbert may have been—or even if he was truly a Christian at all—cannot be determined now. His wife Margaret, however, was a devout and strict Presbyterian. Out on the farm it was difficult to get to church regularly, but she did her best to instill spiritual values in her children.

Gilbert kept his business affairs separate from his family. Even after the children were grown, the family knew little of his occupational pursuits. They only knew that business kept him away all week long and sometimes for several weeks or a month at a time.

In the aftermath of the American Civil War, reconstruction in the South generated an unremitting demand for timber, and Gilbert was especially busy. In the spring of 1878, as he was taking a log raft down river, a larger raft, moving more rapidly in the mainstream, overtook and collided with Gilbert's, knocking the 68-year-old man into the icy waters. He was killed instantly.

If Gilbert left any money, no one in the family knew of it or benefited from it. All that remained was the farm and the hard work that went with it. By then, only one of Gilbert's sons—Jacob—was living at home. Eventually the farm fell into his hands.

Jacob Snyder Tozer married Prudence Jackson, a young girl from a nearby town who knew little of country life. Romance and love brought her to the farm, and the farm introduced her to hard work and, in the course of time, six children.

Aiden Wilson Tozer, born April 21, 1897, was the third.

TOZER-GRAMS

I am fully convinced that no man on earth knows or can know enough to seriously threaten the foundations of our faith. The most that honest scholarship can ever do is to strip away some of the moss that clings to the strong pillars upon which the Church of God rests.

The true follower of Christ will not ask, "If I embrace this truth, what will it cost me?" Rather he

will say, "This is truth. God help me to walk in it, let come what may!"

There are few sadder sights than that of an old man who has outlived his generation and his usefulness, but who, for some reason, still lingers on, staring with crusty disfavor at any servant of the Lord, however humble, who may be for the moment in a place of prominence in the Kingdom of God.

The glory of God is the health of the universe; the essential soundness of things requires that He be honored among created intelligences.

PRAYER

O Lord God Almighty, not the God of the philosophers and the wise but the God of the prophets and apostles; and better than all, the God and Father of our Lord Jesus Christ, may I express Thee unblamed?

They that know Thee not may call upon Thee as other than Thou art, and so worship not Thee but a creature of their own fancy; therefore enlighten our minds that we may know Thee as Thou art, so that we may perfectly love Thee and worthily praise Thee.

In the name of Jesus Christ our Lord. Amen.

"Why We Must Think Rightly about God"
The Knowledge of the Holy

"He impacted my life from childhood days, when I heard him speak at Mahaffey Camp in western Pennsylvania. The truths he expressed in his inimitable style grew stronger and went deeper in my heart as I grew and had opportunity to hear him preach."

Dr. David Rambo
President, The Christian
and Missionary Alliance

3

The Tozertown Farm

The Tozer farm and family were like hundreds of others in hilly, rural western Pennsylvania at the turn of the century. The world was quiet and peaceful. Income taxes had not yet been instituted in the United States. World War 1 had not plunged the world into indescribable chaos.

Though farming in that era generated a limited cash flow, at least it produced all the family needed to eat. On Saturdays, Prudence would take eggs, produce or meat to a nearby store to barter for needed staples such as coffee and sugar. Even so, Prudence Tozer saved pennies to go and hear the famous opera singer, Amelita Galli-Curci. This appreciation for excellence and unwillingness to accept anything but the best contributed to Tozer's subsequent exploration of spiritual things.

An older brother and sister—Zene and Essie—had preceded Aiden in the birth order. Mildred, Margaret and Hugh would follow. As a child, Aiden was rather small and skinny. He displayed a warm affection for his mother, helping her around the house as much as possible.

One of his mother's daily chores was milking the cows—done by hand in those days before electric milking machines. Being small, Aiden was afraid of the cows, especially the ferocious-looking one that had huge curled horns. Aiden did not want to go near that cow if she was looking at him. But the cow with the curled horns had to be milked. It was Aiden's older sister, Essie, who came up with a solution.

"Look, Aiden," Essie explained, "I'll hold the cow by her horns and won't let her look at you. Then you can milk her." The plan worked. By teaming up, the two were able to milk the cow with the funny horns.

Aiden made up for his small stature by antagonizing people. He sometimes would pick a quarrel for no reason at all. His younger sisters received their fair share of his tormenting behavior. Essie usually escaped, perhaps because she was older and quite a bit larger. Aiden was not so sure but that Essie could outdo him if they got into a scrap.

Aiden's antagonizing ways were not limited to the family. His conduct gained him an unsavory reputation among some of the area mothers. Once Aiden and Essie were climbing in an old apple tree that bordered their farm with a neighbor's. Reaching a high, gnarled branch, Aiden began to swing for all he was worth. That feat being insufficiently impressive, he started to sing at the top of his lungs: "Is there any room in heaven/ For a small lad like me?"

As if from heaven, a female voice boomed out of nowhere: "If there's going to be any room for you in heaven, you'll have to mend your ways." The two children, not seeing anyone, were startled into silence. But soon their angry neighbor emerged from the brush. Immediately Aiden recognized her as the mother of his latest victim. What could he do? He was afraid to climb down. Who could tell what this irate mother might do to him? He was not about to find out.

Aiden received a tongue lashing to end all tongue lashings—well deserved, Essie recalled much later. The angry woman finally exhausted herself and went home. Aiden, apparently no worse for the wear, cautiously climbed down. It would take more than a tongue lashing to make an impression on him.

An animal lover

There was another side to Aiden as well. He loved animals. Each year his father raised pigs to sell for Christmas money. One year, the big sow had too many piglets to be accommodated come nursing time. Aiden happened to notice that one of the piglets was not getting much nourishment. Its skin was wrinkled, and its ribs stuck out.

"That little fellow is starving to death," Aiden said to his father. "He's not getting anything to eat!" Aiden walked to the store to purchase a nursing bottle so he could hand-feed "Mickey."

It did not take long for Mickey to become part of the Tozer household. Like a puppy, he followed the children all over the house. When Jacob went out to feed the horses in the morning, along trailed little Mickey, hoping for a handout—an ear of corn or perhaps some horse feed that might spill from the trough. When Prudence would go out to feed the chickens and gather the eggs for the day, the first one to greet her would be Mickey.

"Well, good morning, Mickey," Prudence would say to the pig. And Mickey would squeal in reply, as if to say, "And a good morning to you, too." The "talking pig" soon became a family joke.

Limited schooling

For rural Pennsylvania children at that time, formal schooling was limited. Aiden received a grammar school education at Wood School, named for its pine woods setting. Offered music lessons, but having no talent for music, he deferred to one of his younger sisters. Later, during his teens, he enrolled in a correspondence course in cartooning. Although he did not complete it, he showed considerable promise. Those early sketches reflected the sharpness of his wit, hallmark to all who knew him.

Young Aiden's main source of information was his superstitious, ill-tempered, sharp-tongued, maternal grandmother Jackson. She believed strongly in dreams and consulted her dog-eared dream book for interpretations first thing every morning. She also believed that dog barks were omens of ill-tiding.

In contrast, Aiden's paternal grandmother Tozer often told the children about God, sowing seeds for Aiden's later conversion. She also taught the children that money does not mean everything and that they should get something in their heads.

Life on the Tozer farm was typical of farm life at that time in that region. And the Tozers were a typical, close-knit farm family. They worked together and they played together. They got to know each other well.

But for a young man ambitious to see what was beyond the fences and hills of western Pennsylvania, farm life was more hum-drum and drudgery than exciting. Often Aiden and his sister Essie would sit on a fallen log out behind the barn and plan how they could get away. Not that they did anything about it—then—but talking and planning seemed to relieve their minds.

Sundays, insofar as the chores would allow, were given over to reading and rest. Churches were few and distant; farm work was plentiful and demanding. But Aiden delighted in the Sunday afternoons of reading and read everything he could get his hands on.

Jacob Tozer was in many respects a responsible husband and father, a hard worker and a good provider for his family. With another baby—Hugh, the last—

due in late spring, Jacob wanted to please his wife with something he knew would delight her in the warm days of July and August: a glass of ice water. In 1906, with no refrigeration, ice water in the summer was not easily come by. During the winter, when the streams froze solid, farmers would cut large chunks of ice. These would be packed in fresh sawdust for insulation and stored in the relatively cool spring houses that were on every farm. Jacob made all the necessary preparations, genuinely excited at the thought of surprising his wife.

Alas! When in mid-summer Jacob eagerly went to the spring house to get a piece of the precious ice, he discovered that all of it had melted. At the time, no one realized quite how adversely the disappointment affected Jacob.

There was a much more severe blow the following year. Prudence was baking bread for the family—a process accomplished by first carefully regulating the wood fire in the cook stove. Satisfied that the embers were just right, she put the bread in the oven.

"Essie, dear," she called, recruiting Aiden's older sister, "will you watch my bread while I work in the garden? It should be done in about an hour. Take it out for me then, will you?"

Assured of 14-year-old Essie's cooperation, Prudence went outside to work in her large garden. Meanwhile, Aiden's maternal grandmother, living with the family at the time, came into the kitchen and smelled the bread baking in the oven.

"Ah, Essie," Grandmother remarked, "I see your mother is baking bread."

"Yes, Grandma," Essie replied. "I'm to watch it and take it out when it's finished."

"Is that so?" muttered Grandmother. "I wonder if your mother fixed the fire right. Maybe I should put on some more wood." With that, Grandmother went out to the chopping block and gathered an apronful of pine chips. When she threw the chips on the bed of glowing coals, they burst immediately into intense flame, overheating the chimney and setting fire to the wood shingles on the kitchen roof. Soon the kitchen filled with smoke.

Ten-year-old Aiden, working outside, was suddenly aware of penetrating smoke, curling around the yard, whipped by a brisk wind. He looked up and saw flames dancing on the shingled kitchen roof. He ran for the house just as Essie burst out of the kitchen door.

"Essie!" Aiden yelled. "Do you know this house is on fire?"

"Yes, I know it. Let's get some stuff out of the house. Hurry!"

With that they ran into the house to save as much as they could. By this time, other family members had arrived to lend a hand. About half way up the stairs to the second floor was a small landing. On it Jacob had placed some bags of flour recently processed at the local grist mill.

"Come on, Aiden," Essie yelled. "Help me get this flour out." They each grabbed a corner of a bag and began to drag the 50-pound sack to the safety of the front yard. Both ran back for a second bag. But when they got to the porch, Grandmother met them with some things from her room. "Here, Essie," she cried, "take these out for me." Essie complied, then ran back for another sack of flour. But again Grandmother had another arm load of things rescued from the small upstairs room she occupied. Grandmother kept Essie busy until it was too late to save anything else. The house itself was a total loss.

Meanwhile, Aiden rounded up his two younger sisters and brother and hurried them away to the vantage point of a fallen log down the hill behind the burning house. It was just far enough away to be out of danger but close enough so he could watch what was happening. He made his sisters and brother keep their heads down until it was safe to go back. When one of them would rise up to see the smoke and fire, Aiden would push him or her down.

"Keep your head down!" he warned. "You might get hurt."

According to Essie, Aiden had dreamed about just such a fire. At the time, Essie remembered, he told the family what he planned to do if the house should ever burn. He was prepared.

A new house rose on the old foundations, and the Tozer family remained on the farm five more years. But things were not the same.

Akron bound

Following the fire, Zene, having heard of work in Akron, Ohio, at Goodyear, left home. He was anxious to be on his own. For Jacob, who had recently lost everything in the fire, the departure of his able first-born son was more than he could bear. That fall, Jacob had the first of a number of nervous breakdowns. For most of the winter he was hospitalized with acute depression. In the spring Jacob seemed better and returned home. But over the next several years, he spent more time in the hospital.

Much of the farm responsibility fell on the young shoulders of Aiden, and he borrowed a mule from a neighbor to do the farm work. Years later a sister said of that period, "He was never a boy again."

The children often discussed with their mother the possibility of leaving the farm. Zene reported plenty of work in Akron. Essie and Aiden were both anxious to get city jobs. Prudence could understand the aspirations of her children, but knew how much Jacob loved the farm. Could they convince him to leave it?

Jacob may have been ill, but he was a reasonable man. He realized he probably would never be able to work the farm as he used to and did not want to burden his family with the responsibility. So the decision was made: They would auction the farm for whatever price it would bring and move to Akron.

Aiden, for one, was delighted.

TOZER-GRAMS

While I have no doubt that the grace which has followed me since my boyhood will continue with me while I live on earth and for an eternity after, I have enjoyed already enough of God's benefits to supply me with matter for constant praise for at least

a thousand years to come. If God were to close my account tomorrow and refuse any longer to honor me with His favors, the circumstances of His grace to me so far would require that I should still thank Him unceasingly with tears of honest gratitude.

The warfare of the Christian is like foreign missions, romantic to talk about but drably realistic to live through.

Foxe's Book of Martyrs provides a delightful thrill in the reading, but I doubt that any of the martyrs themselves enjoyed their dying as much as we enjoy reading about them.

The work of Christ on the cross did not influence God to love us, did not increase that love by one degree, did not open any fount of grace or mercy in His heart. He had loved us from eternity, and needed nothing to stimulate that love. The cross is not responsible for God's love; rather it was His love which conceived the cross as the one method by which we could be saved.

PRAYER

Father, I want to know Thee, but my coward heart fears to give up its toys. I cannot part with them without inward bleeding, and I do not try to hide from Thee the terror of the parting. I come trembling, but I do come. Please root from my heart all those things which I have cherished so long and which have become a very part of my living self, so that Thou mayest enter and dwell there without a rival. Then shalt Thou make the place of Thy feet glorious. Then shall my heart have no need of the sun to shine in it, for Thyself wilt be the light of it, and there shall be no night there. In Jesus' Name, Amen.

"The Blessedness of Possessing Nothing"
The Pursuit of God

PERSONAL GLIMPSES

Childhood

When Hugh was still quite small, Aiden took him along to the creek where Aiden and his buddies often swam. Prudence did not allow Hughie to go in the water yet, since he was so little and could not swim.

Aiden had built a small wooden raft from which the boys dove. Placing Hughie in the middle to keep him safe and dry, Aiden began swimming and splashing in the water.

Suddenly Hughie stood up on the wet raft and began sliding off into the water. He began sinking. Aiden's younger sister, Mildred, had come along at that exact moment, fortunately, and leaping in and paddling, she made her way to the spot where the child had gone under.

Soon he popped up, sputtering and wide-eyed. Mildred pulled him to her and headed for the creek bank where she deposited him firmly. In a state of panic she began screaming, "He's dead! I know he's dead!" as Hughie stood shivering, shaking and dripping before her, very much alive.

By this time Aiden had reached the bank and shook her to bring her to her senses. The two of them now faced another dilemma. How could they explain this to their mother?

They were afraid to go home themselves, so they sent little Hughie home alone after drying him off a little. It wasn't far, so he soon arrived home. He was strangely quiet and tried to stay out of sight, but I discovered his damp hair and demanded to know how it had come about. Hughie hung his head ashamedly and said nothing. The story came out finally when much later in the day Aiden and Mildred arrived and were forced to tell the saga of the slippery raft and Hughie's near-drowning.

Essie Tozer Jeffers

Zene loved to race and jump Frances, the fast horse father had raised. When the farm chores were completed, he would take Frances to the road where he had erected makeshift hurdles.

One day Aiden begged Zene to let him try the hurdles. Much against his better judgment and with many misgivings, Zene lifted Aiden up onto the high-strung filly's back and away they went. Unable to control the speed of the horse as Zene had learned to do, Aiden pressed his knees harder and harder into the horse's sides as he clung to stay on.

Frances rose obediently to the occasion and cleared the first hurdle—Aiden did not! He toppled off into a ditch alongside the road, unhurt but shaken and upset. Much needed lessons were hastily given by Zene, and Aiden was soon putting Frances through her paces.

Essie Tozer Jeffers

Aiden often set traps for small animals, but he arranged the box traps in such a way that the animals would not be injured. The lid of the box would drop after the animal was clear and inside. One time he trapped a baby groundhog. Aiden thought the little creature was so cute that he brought it home and the children adopted it as a pet.

The baby groundhog could sit on its haunches and with its forepaws hold bits of food to nibble. This delighted the children. When the groundhog grew a little older and larger, Aiden released it in the field where other groundhogs were often seen.

Essie Tozer Jeffers

Dr. Tozer was raised in the rural areas of La Jose, Pennsylvania, and knew much about nature. Many years later we drove together from Orrville, Ohio, to Nyack, New York. I surprised him by driving to La Jose enroute, where we stayed overnight with relatives. The next morning we drove to the old farm. The home was gone, but the old barn still stood. He took a walk alone, filled with boyhood memories, and then we drove on.

Frank Bertram Miller

❧

On the Sunday I joined church he was an usher and it was he who took me to the front to join. I was a green country girl and was very embarrassed to go with him. I said to a girl I was sitting with, "That was worse than a wedding," which he overheard. Oh, he was a handsome, clean-cut young man of 18 and I was not yet 15.

The young people's group was invited to a pleasant Sunday afternoon in the church parlor, so I went with my girlfriend and it was there that I formally met Aiden Tozer.

Ada Pfautz Tozer

"All who knew him best describe one outstanding characteristic. In a single word it was discipline. Like most mystics down through the ages, Dr. Tozer led a lonely life as men see it; but one of deepest fellowship as he saw it, for he practiced the presence of Christ as few have done in his generation.

"The lessons I learned from the late A.W. Tozer, both from the pulpit and as his part-time associate on the editorial staff of *The Alliance Witness*, will never be forgotten. More than 17 years after his death, I still quote him frequently and pattern many areas of my life after his sterling example."

David Enlow

4

The Pursuit Begins

Akron in 1912 was a busy, bustling city. As a major rubber production center, Akron provided industry—heated by the impending military conflagration that would erupt in Europe—with an essential product.

For Aiden Tozer, Akron was pivotal. Not only did it

mark the end of an era, but it was the locus of important beginnings for a farm boy who, at 15, leaped into manhood.

Aiden's first job, selling candy, peanuts and books as a "butcher boy" on the Vicksburg and Pacific Railroad, was not an auspicious start. He worked on commission, and, because he preferred to sit and read the books he was supposed to be selling, his earnings were negligible. He had an insatiable love for reading and a hearty disinclination for peddling. Selling definitely was not his calling.

He and Essie eventually found jobs at Goodyear. Aiden's job was to hand cut chunks of crude rubber into tiny bits. Aiden worked nights, and as he did very monotonous work with his hands, he would put up a book of poetry in front of him and memorize it as he worked. If the work was tedious, it was less so than farm work in La Jose, Pennsylvania. Memories of the farm were a strong motivation for Aiden to make good at Goodyear.

Besides, for the first time ever, Aiden was earning money of his own. From each pay check he could provide help for the family as well as meet his modest personal needs. The money gave him an air of importance and a sense of independence.

Aiden's father, in his early 50s at the time, still could not handle the stress of regular work. Apart from the proceeds from the sale of the farm, the family was dependent on the children's earnings for its support. To supplement the family income, Prudence boarded some of the young men who had moved to Akron for work in the factories and needed a reputable place to live until they got settled. These boarders afforded young Aiden opportunity to appraise people—a skill he quickly developed. In later life he assessed people almost instinctively, and with uncanny accuracy.

Aiden found Akron exciting and the opportunities stimulating. He even enrolled in high school—for one day. After his introduction to the high school classroom, he felt he could make better progress in independent study. That day terminated his formal education. He achieved his remarkable breadth of knowledge by dint of independent reading and study.

Probably the most significant contribution Akron offered the Tozer family was the opportunity to go to church regularly. Akron did not want for churches. Several were within easy walking distance of the Tozer home. Aiden began attending the nearby Grace Methodist Episcopal Church. He wanted to take his younger sisters, but they complained that they did not have proper clothes for church. So Aiden and Essie took the girls shopping for church clothes. And the next Sunday Aiden was proud to walk into church with his sisters dressed in new outfits.

Conversion experience

Toward the end of his life Tozer reminisced about his conversion experience. "I have thanked God many times for the sweet winsome ways of the Holy Spirit in dealing with the heart of this untaught lad when I was only 17. We had a neighbor by the name of Holman. I do not know his first name or initials. He was just Mr. Holman. He lived next door to us. I had heard that he was a Christian, but he never talked to me about Christ.

"Then one day I was walking up the street with this friendly neighbor. Suddenly, he put his hand on my shoulder. 'You know,' he said, 'I have been wondering about you. I have been wondering if you are a Christian, if you are converted. I just wanted the chance to talk it over with you.'

" 'No, Mr. Holman,' I answered, 'I am not converted, but I thank you for saying this to me. I am going to give it some serious thought.' "

Late one afternoon in 1915—three years after arriving in Akron—as he walked home from work, Aiden noticed a small crowd of people gathered on the opposite side of the street. They were clustered around an older man who seemed to be talking to them. Not being able to hear what the man was saying, Aiden crossed the street to satisfy his curiosity.

At first, the man's speech did not make any sense to Aiden. He spoke with a strong German accent, and Aiden had to listen carefully to catch what the man was saying. Finally, it dawned on Aiden. The man was preaching! Preaching, right out on the street corner! *Doesn't this man have a church to preach in?* Aiden thought to himself. *And it isn't even Sunday! Why is he so excited?* But as Aiden listened, the words of the elderly street preacher began to find their mark in his young heart.

Then the preacher startled Aiden. "If you don't know how to be saved, just call on God, saying, 'God, be merciful to me, a sinner,' and God will hear you."

Those words burned in Aiden's heart. He could not get the voice of the preacher out of his mind. As he slowly walked home, he thought over what the man had said. Never before had he heard words like those. They troubled him. They awakened within him a gnawing hunger for God.

Saved. If you don't know how to be saved . . . just call on God . . . "God, be merciful to me, a sinner."

When Aiden arrived home, he went straight to the attic, where he could be alone to think this out for himself and to wrestle with God. No one knows all that transpired in the Tozer attic that afternoon in 1915. But Aiden Wilson Tozer emerged a new creation in Christ Jesus. His pursuit of God had begun.

Aiden's conversion to Christ was a transforming experience in every way. Inclined to be cynical, he thought nothing of turning to agnostics or even to atheists for counsel. Suddenly, his entire life was radically and wonderfully redirected. A whole new world had opened up to this youth with unbounded intellectual curiosity. It was a world that would take him a lifetime and more to explore fully.

In later years he would say of himself that as a young man he was so ignorant it was a wonder the top of his head did not cave in from sheer emptiness. From the moment of his conversion, however, Aiden had an insatiable thirst for knowledge and a ravenous hunger for God.

The Tozer household was crowded with eight family members plus boarders. Aiden had to find the time and a place to get alone with God, time for prayer and Bible reading and study. In the basement there was a small unused space behind the furnace. Aiden claimed it, cleaned it and made it comfortable. It was a refuge where he could get away from everything and everyone and literally spend hours in prayer, study and meditation.

Long years later Essie remembered how at first, when she would go down the cellar stairs for canned goods, she could hear frightful groanings coming from behind the furnace. Soon she came to recognize the sound as that of her younger brother wrestling with God in prayer. For Aiden, it became a lifetime habit. Nothing would take the place of knowing God firsthand.

An adventurous heart

The desire for firsthand knowledge. Insatiable curiosity. The adventuresome spirit of youth. Those qualities conspired to provide biographers with one of Aiden's more dramatic experiences in life. In fact, it was an experience that almost canceled any need for such a biography.

Soon after his conversion, Aiden and a friend devised a plan to build a raft and float down the river, joining the Ohio and the Mississippi, possibly going as far as New Orleans. It was a Tom Sawyer kind of dream for the two fellows, and they spent many evenings together planning the trip and building the raft. Aiden purposely kept word of this project from his mother. He knew she would never approve such a foolhardy undertaking.

Finally, after weeks of planning and preparation, all

was in readiness. Aiden slipped out of his bedroom window one night to meet his friend down by the river bank. Carefully they packed the raft with everything they would need: extra clothes, a map of the river, ample food. Everything was ready. With adventurous excitement they pushed their craft into the water and scrambled aboard. They were off to see the world.

A reluctant moon slipped out of the clouds to illuminate the liquid highway. The night was still. The river whispered fantastic promises to them. The venture was everything they had dreamed it would be. All night they poled. They were making good time on the peaceful river.

Toward daylight they stopped for breakfast along the riverbank. They fried fresh fish caught that morning from the raft. Could any other circumstance be as exhilarating?

Soon they were back on the raft, continuing their downriver journey. As the sun warmed the morning air and slowly burned the fog off the water, the river became choppy. The farther they traveled downstream, the rougher the water became. It was all the boys could do to keep up with the raft. Their muscles, strained and tired from the night's poling, soon gave way to fatigue. The raft began to spin and the boys lost control of it.

To this point, Aiden and his friend were able to steer clear of dangerous rocks. Now they were at the mercy of the river. With a wrenching thud the raft hit a cluster of rocks, receiving considerable damage. Again they hit rocks, and this time the raft began to break apart, dumping cargo and passengers into the cold waters. Fortunately, both boys were excellent swimmers. As they dragged themselves up the bank of the river, they looked back to see the last of their raft, broken beyond repair, tumbling down the river. Nothing was found of their belongings.

It was a long, silent walk back to Akron. Both were ashamed of their failure. Aiden was so embarrassed that he did not return home immediately. Instead, he located a room across town and found a new job. He did not see how he could face his family. What would he say? How would he say it? He especially did not want to face his mother. He had always had a high regard for her, and would not deliberately do anything to hurt her. How would she react?

Several weeks went by. Aiden purposely avoided everyone who knew him. One day, while walking from work to his lodgings, he turned a corner and ran into Zene, his older brother.

"Is that you, Aiden?" Zene exclaimed in startled unbelief. "Do you know that Mother has been worried sick about you? Where have you been?"

Without giving his younger brother time to respond, Zene continued, "You'd better get yourself home this very day. I'm going to tell Mother that I saw you, and if you're not home soon, I'm coming to find you. Do you understand me, young man?"

Aiden finally returned home. It was, by his own admission, the hardest and most humiliating thing he ever did. It proved, however, to be a good lesson. It enabled him, in his later ministry, to be empathetic with those who had failed. And it was a catharsis of sorts, purging him of interest in material things and their pursuit. From that time forward, Aiden was a different person. He settled down. He sublimated his bent for adventure and his desire for firsthand knowledge to the pursuit of spiritual matters.

These changes in Aiden's life were not lost upon his family. One day, as Aiden's mother was in the kitchen washing dishes, Aiden came upstairs from his basement sanctuary.

"Mother," he began deliberately, "you know that I love you. Ever since I gave my life to Christ, I've been a different person. Wouldn't you like to give your life to Jesus Christ?" Right there in the kitchen he led his mother into a saving relationship with Jesus Christ.

Successively, Aiden also introduced his sisters—those he had tormented as a young boy—to the Lord. They, too, had noted the difference in his life.

Tozer's spiritual pilgrimage was helped along by the nearby Grace Methodist Episcopal Church, where he soon became an active member, although he was baptized in a local Church of the Brethren. The decision to attend Grace Methodist proved fortuitous, for it was there that he met his future wife.

Ada Cecelia Pfautz, a young girl of 15 and fresh from the country, was among several being received into church membership. It was Aiden's assignment to usher her to the front at the proper time for the membership ceremony. Ada was not a little embarrassed to learn that her escort would be a handsome, clean-cut young man still in his teens.

"This is worse than a wedding," Ada whispered to a girlfriend as Aiden reached her pew. He could not help overhear her remark, which further embarrassed the young woman.

Following the morning service, the church youth planned a picnic lunch followed by a Bible study and an afternoon social time in the church parlor. Aiden, never one to pass up an opportunity, invited Ada to attend the gathering with him.

"Oh, no," objected Ada. "I couldn't do that. I have to hurry home; my mother is expecting me."

"Well," persisted Aiden, "there's a telephone over there. Why don't you call your mother and tell her that a very nice young man will be bringing you home later this afternoon?"

Ada laughed. But Aiden's arguments prevailed and Ada did stay and Aiden did take her home that afternoon. In fact, Aiden soon became a regular caller at the Pfautz home.

Ada's background

Ada Cecelia Pfautz was born in 1899. Her parents were farmers in a semirural area of Ohio known as Brittain. Ada's father, Jacob Pfautz, was of German and Swiss ancestry. The Pfautzes were part of the Dunkard church, a German Baptist movement. Members were called Dunkards because of their practice of baptism by immersion. But when Jacob left the Dunkard church, his parents, John and Sarah Pfautz, disinherited him, giving the family farm to Jacob's sister, who remained a Dunkard and married within the church.

Ada's mother, Kate Browning Pfautz, was of Scot-

Irish ancestry. Kate was a descendant of General Rufus Putnam, one of the brothers in command at the battle of Bunker Hill. He later moved west and founded Marietta, Ohio. Kate's father and mother were educated and saw that all their children had at least a high school education. From an early age, Kate developed a strong interest in poetry, writing many poems herself. She had dozens of them published in the local newspapers.

On one corner of the family farm there was a small Methodist church that Kate and Ada regularly attended. It was in that church, during evangelistic meetings, that Ada responded to the "altar call" and committed her life to Jesus Christ.

Like many other area families, the Pfautzes migrated to Akron to take advantage of the industrial boom. The rubber factories were pleading for help, even employing women and children. The Pfautzes moved to Goodyear Heights on Akron's east side, where their employer helped them secure a home of their own.

Kate Pfautz was a deeply religious person who lived the Christian life before her family and witnessed constantly to others. Too constantly, some thought, annoyed by her persistence. Nevertheless, she had a large influence on many people, including A.W. Tozer.

Ada idolized her mother, gave her credit for teaching her everything of value that she knew, and she thought her mother was the model every woman should follow in whatever role she found herself.

Kate seriously prayed that Ada would meet and marry a Christian young man, preferably one headed for the ministry. To young Aiden she took an immediate liking. She made available to him some of her spiritual books. She encouraged him to buy a Scofield Bible and study it diligently.

The filling of the Holy Spirit

It was Kate Pfautz who, a year and a half after his conversion to Christ, prayed with Aiden to be filled with the Holy Spirit.

"Young man," Mrs. Pfautz would say, "you must get down on your knees and die to yourself before the Holy Spirit will fill you." She backed up the statement with detailed instruction and patient persistence. One evening, in her home, Tozer knelt by the sofa and Kate prayed with him. He was instantly filled with the Holy Spirit.

"I was 19 years old," Tozer recalled, "earnestly in prayer, when I was baptized with a mighty infusion of the Holy Spirit." In a later sermon, he told his congregation about the experience.

"I know with assurance what God did for me and within me. At that point, nothing on the outside held any important meaning for me. In desperation and in faith I took a leap away from everything that was unimportant to that which was most important: to be possessed by the Spirit of the living God.

"Any tiny work that God has ever done through me and through my ministry for Him dates back to that hour when I was filled with the Spirit. That is why I plead for the spiritual life of the body of Christ and the eternal ministries of the eternal Spirit through God's children, His instruments."

Tozer would later write extensively on the subject of the filling of the Holy Spirit. In *Keys to the Deeper Life*, he wrote:

> Neither in the Old Testament nor in the New, nor in Christian testimony as found in the writings of the saints as far as my knowledge goes was any believer ever filled with the Holy Spirit who did not know he had been filled. Neither was anyone filled who did not know when he was filled. And no one was ever filled gradually.
>
> Behind these three trees many half-hearted souls have tried to hide like Adam from the presence of the Lord, but they are not good enough hiding places: The man who does not know when he was filled was never filled (though of course it is possible to forget the date). And the man who hopes to be filled gradually will never be filled at all.

What mother would not be happy to welcome such a son-in-law into the household? On April 26, 1918, three years after Aiden and Ada first met, and five days after his 21st birthday, Aiden Wilson Tozer and Ada Cecelia Pfautz became husband and wife.

TOZER-GRAMS

There is one sure way to escape the delusions of religion: Receive Christ as Lord of our lives and begin to obey Him in everything. Submit to the

truth and let it search us. Submit and obey are hard and exacting words; but necessary if we would be true Christians.

✥

The man of true faith may live in the absolute assurance that his steps are ordered by the Lord. For him misfortune is outside the bounds of possibility. He cannot be torn from this earth one hour ahead of the time which God has appointed, and he cannot be detained on earth one moment after God is done with him here. He is not a waif of the wide world, a foundling of time and space, but a saint of the Lord and the darling of His particular care.

✥

Much unworthy thinking has been done about the cross, and a lot of injurious teaching has resulted. The idea that Christ rushed in breathless to catch the upraised arm of God ready to descend in fury upon us is not drawn from the Bible. It has arisen from the necessary limitations of human speech in attempting to set forth the fathomless mystery of atonement.

✥

We have been redeemed not by one Person of the Trinity pitting Himself against another, but by the three Persons working in the ancient and glorious harmony of the Godhead.

✥

Our chief difficulty in dealing with God is the habit of trying to make our own terms instead of meeting the terms already laid down. With our mouths we sturdily deny that weeping has any value,

but I fear that in our hearts we are often guilty of embracing the heresy of tears. We sometimes allow our natural sympathy to throw us over on the side of rebellious humanity against God Himself.

PRAYER

O God, quicken to life every power within me, that I may lay hold on eternal things. Open my eyes that I may see; give me acute spiritual perception; enable me to taste Thee and know that Thou art good. Make heaven more real to me than any earthly thing has ever been. Amen.

"Apprehending God"
The Pursuit of God

"Growing up under the ministry of A.W. Tozer on Chicago's southside has left its imprint on me. An appreciation of quiet worship. A hunger to know God. A love for the great hymns and the devotional classics of the Church. A dissatisfaction with most preaching, including my own."

Rev. David Moore
Vice President of Overseas Ministries
The Christian and Missionary Alliance

5

Tozer Begins to Preach

As Aiden Tozer and Ada Pfautz voiced their vows at Grace Methodist Episcopal Church in Akron, April 26, 1918, there was little about the bridegroom to suggest his future worldwide reputation as a minister of the gospel and respected Christian writer. His formal education was rudimentary at best. His English was poor and laced with western Pennsylvania colloquialisms. He was still a factory worker at Goodyear. Ada fully expected that factory work would always be the family's livelihood.

Already the young man had hinted of other things. Prior to his marriage, Aiden took leave of his factory job to go with his sister Essie's husband, John S. Jeffers, to Mount Pleasant, West Virginia, on a preaching mission of several weeks. Many claimed to have been born again. A month and a half after his marriage, Aiden and his brother-in-law returned to Mount Pleasant, this time with Ada. They spent the entire summer in door-to-door evangelism, preaching almost every night of the week in school houses scattered throughout the mountains. They also held tent meetings in Huntington. For young Aiden Tozer and his bride, it was a heady experience, with many people turning to Christ through the team's ministry.

"Aiden was quite new in the faith," Ada remembered, "and with little formal schooling he was entirely dependent on the Lord."

Both their plans and their spirits were abruptly dashed when Aiden received a summons to report for military duty. Although the armistice of World War 1 was only months away, no one could forecast that fact with certainty. Aiden's orders were to report to an army camp in Chillicothe, Ohio, for induction.

The Tozers had no money beyond pocket change. And what would Ada do in West Virginia while her husband was in the service of his country?

"At first it appeared I would be left behind," Ada recalled. "I was still only 18, and I insisted that I must go to Mother's."

Through the generosity of local Christians, they managed to buy two train tickets: one to Chillicothe for Aiden and one to Akron for Ada. It was a trip memorable for its misery. They sat up all night, first on the train and then in Kenowa, Ohio, waiting for their connection. "When we arrived at the old Baltimore and Ohio station in Akron," Ada remembers, "we said our goodbyes, and Aiden continued to Chillicothe. I arrived penniless at Mother's, and had to get work immediately."

Military service turned out to be but a brief stint for Aiden. The armistice was signed on November 11, and Aiden was discharged from duty in time to be home for Christmas. By that time Kate and some others had started a small pentecostal mission church in her community of Newton Heights. Mrs. Pfautz invited her son-in-law to occasionally fill the pulpit.

Early preaching development

Aiden's development as a preacher pleased Ada. "I encouraged my husband all I could," she commented. "I thought he was wonderful. His English was still poor, and he still used his Pennsylvania colloquialisms. But the people did not seem to mind."

By this time Aiden was an active street preacher as well. Nearly every evening found him involved in street meetings. If his sermons were not models of good English, at least he was beginning his ministry, and gaining valuable experience.

But not in the thinking of Grace Methodist Episcopal Church. They were not particularly pleased with the direction Aiden Wilson Tozer was setting for himself. Not that the church was opposed to evangelism or to one of its members entering the ministry, but the street was hardly the place for evangelism, and those aspiring to gospel ministry should go the route of college and seminary.

Meanwhile, Tozer had encountered some street evangelists who said they were members of the nearby Christian and Missionary Alliance church. The name was a tongue-twister, he decided, but the members were extremely interested in evangelism—just as he was. Several teams from the church were regularly out on street corners doing what he and some of his friends were doing. Aiden and Ada decided to visit the church. There they met the pastor, Rev. Samuel M. Gerow, who organized the church youth into evangelistic teams that conducted street meetings throughout the city.

On the way home, Aiden announced to Ada, "That's the church we'll be going to from now on. I like it." And that settled the matter.

Soon both Aiden and Ada were active participants in the life and ministry of The Christian and Missionary Alliance. They also began to hear some teaching that they had not heard at Grace Methodist. They heard expressions such as "The Fourfold Gospel"—Jesus Christ: Savior, Sanctifier, Healer and Coming King—and "The Deeper Life." Both young people were hungry for God. They drank in this fresh biblical teaching with rapturous delight. Pastor Gerow permitted young Tozer to read books from his library and had him preach in his church.

For its part, the church saw in Aiden and his wife a serious young Christian couple. They gave them every possible encouragement. At the time there was considerable interest within the Alliance to begin branch churches. New churches required pastors. The Alliance seemed to be always looking for likely prospects. It was not long until the Akron church leaders recommended Aiden as a pastoral candidate to Rev. Harry M. Shuman, the superintendent for the central region of the United States.

West Virginia bound

The Stonewood Christian and Missionary Alliance Church in West Virginia was looking for a young pastor at the time. The church was started in 1916 by Rev. Robert J. Cunningham, a former Irish missionary to Africa. In the summer of 1916 he pitched a tent in the Clarksburg area and as a result of his evangelistic labors a church was started. The congregation constructed a small one-room building without a basement for their church.

Rev. Cunningham heard about young Tozer from Rev. Shuman, who recommended him for the church. Cunningham invited Tozer to come to the Stonewood church for a two-week evangelistic campaign. Although Tozer had never attended a Bible school or college, the people found him to be truly on fire for the Lord and possessed by a passion for soul winning. His evangelistic endeavors were fruitful. At the conclusion of the two weeks the congregation extended to Tozer an invitation to become pastor of the church. He accepted the appointment and began his ministry in The Christian and Missionary Alliance.

And, true to form, he accepted the appointment without reference to Ada back in Akron.

"He went with no hesitation about leaving me at my mother's and working," said Ada. "But I wrote him alerting him to the fact that as soon as I could get things arranged at home with my parents, I would be joining him in Clarksburg."

If growth was not spectacular, at least the efforts of the minister attracted the attention of the Alliance congregation in Morgantown. At the time, the Morgantown church was also small, but it was larger than Clarksburg and the potential for growth was far greater. They had just completed a building program and were ready for an aggressive evangelistic ministry to the area. In 1921 the Morgantown Christian and Missionary Alliance Church extended a call to Tozer, and he accepted. He began his ministry there on December 4, 1921.

In keeping with the walk-by-faith philosophy, many Alliance churches in those days provided financially for their pastors not as a matter of budget but by what they called a freewill offering. Members segregated part of their weekly tithes and offerings and designated that part for the support of their pastor. That aggregate sum was what the pastor and his family lived on for the ensuing week.

The Tozer family, augmented by then with the first of what eventually would be six boys and a girl, had to pray and trust God for food to eat. God always came through. A parishioner would stop by the parsonage with a small bag of groceries, and the Tozer family would thank God and eat once more. Times were hard, but Aiden Tozer was in his glory. He was doing what God had called him to do. How could obeying God be a hardship? Did He not promise to supply a Christian's every need?

"Any of us," Tozer once wrote, "who have experienced a life and ministry of faith can relate how the Lord has met our needs. My wife and I would probably have starved in those early years of ministry if we could not have trusted God completely for food and everything else. Of course, we are convinced that God can send money to His believing children—but it becomes a pretty cheap thing to get excited about the money and fail to give the glory to Him who is the Giver!"

Those lessons of faith and trust, learned early in his ministry, would prove invaluable in the years ahead. They also determined an attitude toward money and material things from which Tozer would not deviate throughout his life. Having food and clothing, he was content.

Tozer never became rich from his writings—or from any of his other ministries. He signed away much of the book royalties he might have received. Even in the peak years of his pastoral ministry, his salary was meager—not because the church was unwilling to do better but because Tozer considered what he received enough. When he was given honoraria for his outside speaking engagements, he likely as not gave the money away to worthy causes. Many years later when the matter of salary increase came before the church board, Tozer asked to leave the room. Before leaving he reminded the board that his family had all they needed—the board little realized how needy they really were.

The Christian and Missionary Alliance, in addition to its peculiar way of compensating many of its pastors in the earlier years, had another practice that is still followed. It ordained its ministers after first proving them in two or more years of on-the-job experience.

After a year at Stonewood, Tozer met with the district licensing and ordaining council. There were preachers on the council who did not see much potential in this young preacher from the mountains of West Virginia. But they gave him the benefit of the doubt. On August 18, 1920, at the Beulah Beach Bible Conference Center west of Cleveland, the ordaining council set Aiden Wilson Tozer apart for the gospel ministry.

Ordination covenant

Tozer did not take his ordination lightly. Afterwards he found a place of solitude on the old campground and there poured out his heart to God in reflection and prayer. The covenant he made before God on that occasion he later formalized and published in one of the first issues of *Alliance Life* he edited:

O Lord, I have heard Thy voice and was afraid. Thou hast called me to an awesome task in a grave and perilous hour. Thou art about to shake all nations and the earth and also heaven, that the things that cannot be shaken may remain.

O Lord, my Lord, Thou hast stooped to honor me to be Thy servant. No man taketh this honor upon himself save he who is called of God, as was Aaron. Thou hast ordained me Thy messenger to them that are stubborn of heart and hard of hearing. They have rejected Thee, the Master, and it is not to be expected that they will receive me, the servant.

My God, I shall not waste time deploring my weakness or my unfitness for this work. The responsibility is not mine, but Thine. Thou hast said, "I knew thee—I ordained thee—I sanctified thee," and Thou hast also said, "Thou shalt go to all that I shall send thee, and whatsoever I command thee thou shalt speak." Who am I to argue with Thee or to call into question Thy sovereign choice? The decision is not mine but Thine. So be it, Lord. Thy will, not mine, be done.

Well do I know, Thou God of the prophets and the apostles, that as long as I honor Thee Thou wilt honor me. Help me therefore to take this solemn vow to honor Thee all my future life and labors, whether by gain or by loss, by life or by death, and then to keep that vow unbroken while I live.

It is time, O God, for Thee to work, for the enemy has entered into Thy pastures and the sheep are torn and scattered. And false shepherds abound who deny the danger and laugh at the perils that surround Thy flock. The sheep are deceived by these hirelings and follow them with touching loyalty while the wolf closes in to kill and destroy. I beseech Thee, give me sharp eyes to detect the presence of the enemy; give me understanding to see and courage to report what I see faithfully. Make my voice so like Thine own that even the sick sheep will recognize it and follow Thee.

Lord Jesus, I come to Thee for spiritual preparation. Lay Thy hand upon me. Anoint me with the oil of the New Testament prophet. Forbid that I should become a religious scribe and thus lose my prophetic calling. Save me from the curse that lies dark across the face of the modern clergy, the curse of compromise, of imitation, of professionalism. Save me from the error of judging a church by its size, its popularity or the amount of its yearly offerings. Help me to remember that I am a prophet—not a promoter, not a religious manager, but a prophet. Let me never become a slave to crowds. Heal my soul of carnal ambitions and deliver me from the itch for publicity. Save me from bondage to things. Let me not waste my days puttering around the house. Lay Thy terror upon me, O God, and drive me to the place of prayer where I may wrestle with principalities and powers and the rulers of the darkness of this world. Deliver me from overeating and late sleeping. Teach me self-discipline that I may be a good soldier of Jesus Christ.

I accept hard work and small rewards in this life. I ask for no easy place. I shall try to be blind to the little ways that could make my life easier. If others seek the smoother path, I shall try to take the hard way without judging them too harshly. I shall expect opposition and try to take it quietly when it comes. Or if, as sometimes it falleth out to Thy servants, I should have grateful gifts pressed upon me by Thy kindly people, stand by me then and save me from the blight that often follows. Teach me to use whatever I receive in such manner that it will not injure my soul or diminish my spiritual power.

If in Thy permissive providence honor should come to me from Thy church, let me not forget in that hour that I am unworthy of the least of Thy mercies and that if men knew me as intimately as I know myself they would withhold their honors or bestow them upon others more worthy to receive them.

And now, O Lord of heaven and earth, I consecrate my remaining days to Thee; let them be many or few, as Thou wilt. Let me stand before the great or minister to the poor and lowly. That choice is not mine, and I would not influence it if I could. I am Thy servant to do Thy will, and that will is sweeter to me than position or riches or fame. I choose it above all things on earth or in heaven.

Although I am chosen of Thee and honored by a high and holy calling, let me never forget that I am but a man of dust and ashes, a man with all the natural faults and passions that plague the race of men. I pray Thee, therefore, my Lord and Redeemer, save me from myself and from all the injuries I may do myself while trying to be a blessing to others. Fill me with Thy power by the Holy Spirit, and I will go in Thy strength and tell of Thy righteousness, even Thine only. I will spread abroad the message of redeeming love while my normal powers endure.

Then, dear Lord, when I am old and weary and too tired to go on, have a place ready for me above and make me to be numbered with Thy saints in glory everlasting.

Amen.

TOZER-GRAMS

Most Christians, I find, help each other very little in ordinary conversation, and often do each other much harm. There are few who can talk for any length of time without descending to speech that is not only unprofitable but positively harmful.

For myself, I get little help from the fellowship of Christians, and I am sure that up to this time they have received very little help from mine.

A few preachers have found a happy solution to the economic problem in the simple plan of living by faith. No one can put the economic squeeze on such a man; for as he is accountable to God alone for his ministry. God is, by the same token, responsible for his daily bread. It is impossible to starve a man into submission under this arrangement, for the servant of God lives on manna, and manna can be found wherever faith can see it.

If we would but quickly surrender to the will of God we could the sooner begin to enjoy His blessings.

PRAYER

Lord, teach me to listen. The times are noisy and my ears are weary with the thousand raucous sounds which continuously assault them. Give me the spirit of the boy

Samuel when he said to Thee, "Speak, for Thy servant heareth." Let me hear Thee speaking in my heart. Let me get used to the sound of Thy Voice, that its tones may be familiar when the sounds of earth die away and the only sound will be the music of Thy speaking Voice. Amen.

"The Speaking Voice"
The Pursuit of God

"A.W. Tozer was a true, modern-day prophet. He feared no group or individual, and spoke directly to the conscience and the will of his listeners. To judge by his written comments in the *Alliance Weekly* and elsewhere, one might suspect that he rather enjoyed writing in 'the accusative case,' but, tart comments and all, he was more often right than wrong."

Dr. Robert A. Cook
Interim Executive Director
National Religious Broadcasters

6

Indianapolis—Apprenticeship in Earnest

From Morgantown, West Virginia, A.W. Tozer went to the East Side Chapel of The Christian and Missionary Alliance in Toledo, Ohio, ministering there for some time until 1924. He continued his practice of evangelism within his community and regularly accepted invitations to preach in other churches. Summer Bible conferences were becoming popular in the denomination, and Tozer often served as youth evangelist at these gatherings.

Possibly the most significant event of Tozer's short Toledo ministry was a visit from his father. Tozer's memories of his father were not especially happy ones. Jacob Tozer had been a strict disciplinarian, and Aiden had been under the rod more times than he cared to remember. Then, during Aiden's teens, his father suffered the nervous breakdown that hospitalized him for long periods and made it impossible for him to support his family. This put pressure on everyone else, especially on his wife, Aiden's mother.

Although Tozer had introduced his mother and, subsequently, other family members to the Savior, Jacob Tozer remained outside the fold. Then, while Tozer was pastor in Toledo, his father came to hear him preach. Immediately he was impressed. He liked what he heard. When at the end of the service Aiden invited people to come forward and publicly receive Christ, his father rose from his seat, knelt at the front of the church and gave his life to Christ.

The transformation was immediate and remarkable. From that moment, he was a changed man. His daughters, Tozer's sisters, remember how after that he was always humming a hymn. "When the Roll Is Called Up Yonder" was his favorite. That was the song sung at his funeral several years later.

December, 1924, proved a significant milestone in Tozer's life. He began a four-year ministry at the Indianapolis, Indiana, Alliance church. In cooperation with a neighboring Alliance church, the church published a monthly newsletter for its members. The

January 1925 issue announced the Indianapolis church's new pastor:

"Rev. A.W. Tozer has been called to the pastorate of the Indianapolis church of the Alliance. Rev. Tozer, having accepted the call, preached his first sermon as our new pastor on Sunday morning, December 7.

"Rev. Tozer, while young in years, is mature in faith and wisdom and comes to us highly recommended by our district superintendent, Rev. H.M. Shuman, and by our former pastor, Rev. Albert Greenwald. The official board of the local church feels that the church is very fortunate in securing the services of Rev. Tozer, for he possesses that three-fold qualification that every minister should have: the power of the indwelling Holy Spirit, an intimate knowledge of the Bible and the ability to forcefully present the things which be of God."

The words may have been dutifully hammered out by a church secretary or perhaps by the chairman of the pulpit committee, glad that his burdensome responsibility was over, but they accurately reflected the feelings of the Indianapolis congregation. The people genuinely liked their cerebral, reflective young minister.

Until Indianapolis, each of Tozer's congregations had been small. Consequently, Tozer had focused a good share of his attention on the unchurched of the community. Most of his preaching had been evangelistic. His model had been Paul Rader, a dynamic turn-of-the-century evangelist who had followed Dr. A.B. Simpson, as president of The Christian and Missionary Alliance. Tozer heard Rader preach on numerous occasions; to a certain extent he had picked up not only Rader's evangelistic burden but Rader's distinct style of preaching.

Indianapolis was different. The congregation was substantial. The people expected their pastor-shepherd to feed them week after week through his sermons. This ministry demanded that he search the Scriptures and expose himself to God in order to share the riches of God with his people.

Tozer still received invitations to speak. But with increasing frequency, the requests were not for a series of evangelistic or youth sermons, but for a Bible-teaching ministry. The focus of his ministry was definitely shifting—or, more accurately, was being shifted.

It was at Indianapolis that the study habits Tozer established at his conversion began to pay dividends. Radio was not yet invented; television was undreamed of. Much of the time Tozer was not working was spent in the pursuit of God. As far as he was concerned, there was no substitute for knowing God firsthand. He brought the same attitude to knowledge in general. Tozer possessed an intellectual appetite that was not easily satisfied. He developed a remarkable program of self-education and read voraciously and widely. His breadth of knowledge was wrested single-handedly from the books he read.

Trips to the library

Those who remember those days remember his regular trips to the public library. Every Monday and

Wednesday people would see Tozer walking to the library with both arms loaded with books. He would exchange those books and return with a similar load. When parishioners visited the parsonage the young pastor would be in his upstairs study. One church member reflected, "You could tear the house down and Tozer wouldn't know it." He was committed to study and prayer. In fact, some people were fearful for him. They thought his studious pursuits would destroy him.

Raymond McAfee remembered Tozer telling him about those early days. Some of his contemporary Alliance ministers thought that he had gone off the deep end, and often they would chide him about this. "Tozer would smile," McAfee reflected, "when he would talk about this and say, 'Now they want to hear me preach.' "

What set Tozer apart was his ability to quickly assimilate the knowledge he gained from reading. Tozer was more than a reader—he was a thinker. He often counseled, "You should think 10 times more than you read." This was his own practice throughout his life. By doing his own thinking, he arrived at his own independent conclusions. As one member reflected on that period of Tozer's ministry, "He could say more in 15 minutes than many preachers could say in an hour."

The emphasis of Tozer's ministry was changing, but that did not signal an abandonment of his early love for evangelistic preaching. He found many opportunities for such ministry in Indianapolis. He and a neighboring Alliance pastor, Rev. Frank Bertram

Miller, frequently teamed up to hold open-air meetings at various factories throughout the city during the lunch hour. The experience was excellent training for both young men.

Many of the factory workers delighted to heckle the young preachers while they were speaking, hoping to unnerve them with a comment or a question. Admittedly, Tozer at first found it intimidating. But his quick wit came to the rescue. Soon he found himself delighting in the contest and able to field about every remark tossed at him.

During his Indianapolis years, Tozer found himself increasingly influenced by Rev. Edward D. "Daddy" Whiteside, called "the praying man of Pittsburgh." Whiteside was so given to prayer that he was known more for his praying than his preaching. He discipled scores of young men whom he sent out to establish churches throughout southwestern Pennsylvania. His influence at the time was remarkable; in retrospect, it was incalculable. Tozer was impelled by this godly man's prayer life. When Whiteside died on August 8, 1927, Tozer spent a whole week in mourning.

Not only in his preaching did the Indianapolis situation force Tozer to develop the pulpit ministry for which he later would be so well known, but he was also challenged to begin writing. The monthly church newsletter, *The Light of Life,* that had announced his arrival was accustomed to printing a pastoral sermon in each issue. This assignment demanded that he set down his thoughts in formal prose. Over these written sermons he labored, testing each word, making sure the impact was as hard-hitting as he could make it.

Thus he honed the writing skills that would later earn him a place in Christian history.

"Tozer-grams" begin

The monthly newsletter soon added a new feature: "Tozer-grams." These were pithy sayings gleaned from Tozer's pulpit ministry or reflections from his hours in his study. These "Tozer-grams" quickly became a favorite feature of the newsletter. Other district pastors and churches were eager for copies. Circulation increased.

The popularity of the publication evoked rumblings of displeasure from a few pastors within the district who viewed it as competition to the official publication of The Christian and Missionary Alliance, at the time called *The Alliance Weekly,* now *Alliance Life.* Fatuous though the argument was, it introduced Tozer to the sniping that eventually he would know only too well.

The Indianapolis Alliance congregation responded enthusiastically to Tozer's ministry, and Tozer reciprocated. He was an ambitious pastor, with lofty aspirations of what he wanted to do for God. He was pleased to see the church enjoying steady growth. His family was also growing. By this time he had a parsonage full of boys. Tozer liked Indianapolis, and he liked his people. For all he knew, he might remain there the rest of his life.

Not that there were no ripples on the sea of tranquility. One of them seemed to be of typhoon proportion. A member of the congregation "who had lots of money and very little sense," Tozer recalled, left the church and built another just around the corner. "He said he had nothing against me; he just wanted a bigger church—one that was going somewhere."

Tozer smarted under the insinuation that he was not doing an adequate job. "I was a very young preacher," Tozer confessed, "and I went to God in tears. I wanted to know why this was happening to me."

God directed Tozer to Exodus 23 and God's assurance to Israel that He would bring them to the land He had prepared. "I will be an enemy to your enemies and will oppose those who oppose you," God said to Israel (verse 22). "But," God continued, "I will not drive them out in a single year. . . . Little by little I will drive them out before you, until you have increased enough to take possession of the land" (verse 30).

It was as though God was saying, "Son, if I give you a big wide ministry right away, you will blow up. So I will take you a little at a time, and I will enlarge you a little at a time."

From that hour, Tozer saw an increase in his ministry. Out of the crucible of that experience he wrote what later became known as "Five Vows for Spiritual Power."

And the other church and the wealthy man eager to see his church really go somewhere? "It went somewhere, all right," Tozer added. "Right into the ground."

TOZER-GRAMS

The minister himself should simply carry into the pulpit on Sunday the same spirit which has characterized him all week long. He should not need to adopt another voice nor speak in a different tone. The subject matter would necessarily differ from that of his ordinary conversation, but the mood and attitude expressed in his sermons should be identical with his daily living.

Apart from prayer there is probably no Bible doctrine which receives so much attention as does faith, yet there are few things about which we know less.

One trouble with us today is that we know too many things.

The whole trend of the moment is toward the accumulation of a multitude of unrelated facts without a unifying philosophy to give them meaning.

The neat little digest magazines tend to encourage faith in the idea-hopping type of study. This produces an informed superficiality worse in many ways than ignorance itself.

The prophets and reformers of the past were men of few but mighty convictions. Their very narrowness secured high compression and gave added power to their lives.

PRAYER

Lord, how excellent are Thy ways, and how devious and dark are the ways of man. Show us how to die, that we may rise again to newness of life. Rend the veil of our self-life from the top down as Thou didst rend the veil of the Temple. We would draw near in full assurance of faith. We would dwell with Thee in daily experience here on this earth so that we may be accustomed to the glory when we enter Thy heaven to dwell with Thee there. In Jesus' name, Amen.

"Removing the Veil"
The Pursuit of God

"It was with fear and intimidation that I entered his office on the day of my appointment. The office was not what I expected at all. It was not very big and rather dingy and not too well furnished. It had the appearance of being lived in. He was dressed in a suit with a sweater on under his suit coat, which was generally his stock and trade.

"He had a kind and gracious spirit and we visited together. He asked me about the work and within moments I felt very much at home. My fear of A.W. Tozer had left me for good. From that point on I saw him as a man of God, one that I could relate to and approach."

Dr. Keith M. Bailey
District Superintendent,
The Christian and Missionary Alliance

7

A Reluctant Candidate

The Christian and Missionary Alliance, the church denomination under which A.W. Tozer served and which he profoundly influenced, had its organizational start in Maine. At the time, Canadian-born founder Albert B. Simpson was the pastor of an independent church, The Gospel Tabernacle, in New York City. With few exceptions, the new denomination was limited to the Northeast, with Toronto-New York its axis.

When, following the death of Simpson, Chicago-based Paul Rader became president, he encouraged the 32-year-old Alliance to expand westward. He appointed Robert R. Brown, a flamboyant preacher with a passion for missions and evangelism, as superintendent of the Western District. The Western District encompassed all of the United States west of the Mississippi. Only R.R. Brown could have taken such an assignment seriously.

(Later, Brown would gain international fame as the first religious broadcaster on radio—April 8, 1923, on WOW, Omaha, Nebraska, sponsored by Woodmen of the World Insurance. His program went on to become the longest continuous radio program, religious or secular, on any one station in the world.)

One of Brown's first actions as superintendent was to establish a Christian and Missionary Alliance congregation in Chicago. He rented Normal College Auditorium and, assisted by C.L. Eicher and other missionaries, conducted six weeks of meetings. The Chicago Alliance officially organized on March 2, 1922, with Brown serving briefly as its first leader. He was followed by H.W. Ferrin (1922–24), H.F. Meltzer (1924–26) and Joseph Hogue (1927–28). The group bought a large garage on the Southside and remodeled it into a tabernacle. The Southside Gospel

Tabernacle of Chicago, as it was called then, grew to around 80 congregants—at the time a sizable gathering for the Alliance.

Typical of most Alliance groups at the time, the Sunday services were confined to Sunday afternoon and evening so as not to conflict with the morning activities of the denominational churches. The Alliance did not then look upon itself as a church denomination. Rather, it sought the participation of Christians from all denominations who shared its concern for world missions and desired a closer walk with God. Many of its adherents still belonged to one or another of the denominational churches and attended their church services regularly.

With the departure of Joseph Hogue in 1928, the Southside Gospel Tabernacle was without a pastor. Superintendent Brown, faced with the responsibility of filling the vacancy, thought immediately of young Aiden Tozer. He and Tozer had crossed paths at some of the Alliance conventions. Tozer's preaching impressed Brown. Although the two men could not have been more different, they had become friends. Brown's recommendation of Tozer to the Chicago congregation struck fire with a young couple in the church who had heard him speak at a summer Bible conference.

The church sent several letters to Tozer in Indianapolis inviting him to consider being their pastor. But the Indianapolis church was prospering, the people were good to their young pastor, and Tozer had no desire to make a change. He tossed the letters in the waste basket.

Persistence pays off

The Chicago people, however, were persistent. They kept sending letters to Tozer. Finally, he agreed to go to Chicago for a Sunday and preach at Southside Gospel Tabernacle.

It was a hot summer Sunday afternoon. Tozer arrived just prior to the three o'clock worship service. J. Francis Chase, a professional commercial artist, was chairman of the meeting. The two men shook hands, Chase briefed Tozer on the order of service, and the two went to the platform to begin the meeting.

"A.W. Tozer did not make an imposing appearance," Chase later recalled. "He was rather slight in appearance with lots of black hair. His shoes were high-backed, with hooks starting half way up the front. He wore a narrow black tie. Especially by Chicago standards, he was not a fashionable dresser."

When it came time for Tozer to speak, he rose from his chair and stepped to the pulpit. Omitting any niceties, like being happy to be there, he announced his sermon topic: "God's Westminster Abbey." He took his text from Hebrews 11.

The people soon forgot about his appearance as they became caught up in the sermon. Here was a fresh approach to preaching as far as they were concerned. His splendid voice and diction charmed them. This man used superior language and phrases—simple and at the same time grand. And the content—he was feeding their souls.

Everyone was profoundly affected. Following the

service, older members of the church whispered to board members, "Don't let him get away!"

But the congregation's enthusiasm was not reciprocated. United States President Calvin Coolidge had just declined to run for another term of office with the cryptic, headline-making announcement, "I do not choose to run." When Tozer had the inevitable session with the church committee after the service, he told them, "I do not choose to run."

The evening service proved as remarkable as the afternoon worship hour. Tozer's topic was "The Resurrection of the Dead." His sermon confirmed to the people that this preacher was the man for their church. His services must be secured at any cost.

Just what finally convinced Tozer to move to Chicago may never be known. Certainly, he sensed that his ministry was gradually taking on new directions and a new dimension. Perhaps he looked on Chicago as a part of that change. He went to Chicago again, this time with more of an open mind. He preached. He spent some time looking for suitable housing for his growing family. He met again with the church board.

In his meeting with the board, Tozer made the priorities of his ministry clear. He was not a visiting pastor. He believed his ministry required hours of study, prayer and meditation each day. If he was to feed the flock on Sundays, he could not spend all week visiting them in their homes.

The conditions laid down by Tozer were unusual, but the board continued to believe he was the man their church needed. After considerable discussion and prayer, the board agreed to Tozer's stipulations and issued him an official call. Tozer accepted.

The church was delighted. Immediately, they sent notice to everyone on the mailing list: "He was elected, has accepted, and will be here on November 4, 1928, and he is called Rev. A.W. Tozer, the man from Indianapolis."

But the man from Indianapolis was still shadowed by doubts. The genuine regret at Indianapolis when he tendered his resignation did not help his peace of mind. Had he been premature? He was uneasy in spirit, not sure he was doing the right thing.

The family packed for the move, but without enthusiasm. Finally, Tozer loaded wife, sons and luggage into his 1925 Oakland and with a final backward glance at the Indianapolis parsonage they were on their way to Chicago.

"As soon as I had passed the city limits of Indianapolis," Tozer confided years later to Francis Chase, "I had a favorable earnest in my spirit concerning my decision. There swept over my soul a sweet peace. I knew that I was in the will of God."

Tozer and his divinely ordered destiny were about to link up.

TOZER-GRAMS

In baseball a player always goes back and sits down after he strikes out. It would help matters in many a church if that rule could be applied to board members.

A preacher not long ago announced that he would have for his subject the next Sunday evening, "Don't Tear Your Shirt." He took for his text these words, "Rend your hearts and not your garments," and preached on repentance. It is that kind of thing that makes atheists. To approach a solemn subject in such a flippant manner is inexcusable. It is time the Christian public goes on a gracious and dignified strike against such comic-strip parody of gospel preaching. A listener said of Moody, "He was the most deadly in earnest man I ever heard." He adorned the message he preached.

A church can wither as surely under the ministry of soulless Bible exposition as it can where no Bible at all is given. To be effective the preacher's message must be alive; it must alarm, arouse, challenge. It must be God's present voice to a particular people. Then, and not till then, is it the prophetic word and the man himself a prophet.

PRAYER

Glory be to God on high. We praise Thee, we bless Thee, we worship Thee for Thy great glory. Lord, I uttered that I understood not; things too wonderful for me which I knew not. I heard of Thee by the hearing of the ear, but now mine eye seeth Thee and I abhor myself in dust and ashes. O Lord, I will lay my hand upon my mouth. Once have I spoken, yea, twice, but I will proceed no further.

But while I was musing the fire burned. Lord, I must speak of Thee, lest by my silence I offend against the generation of Thy children. Behold, Thou hast chosen the foolish things of the world to confound the wise, and the weak things of the world to confound the mighty. O Lord, forsake me not. Let me show forth Thy strength unto this generation and Thy power to everyone that is to come. Raise up prophets and seers in Thy Church who shall magnify Thy glory and through Thine almighty Spirit restore to Thy people the knowledge of the holy. Amen.

"The Holiness of God"
The Knowledge of the Holy

PERSONAL GLIMPSES

The Personal Side

When preparing to leave the Beulah Beach conference grounds to proceed to a speaking engagement, I met Dr. Tozer on my way out.

"Where are you going?" he asked.

I replied, "To the Okoboji conference." I then added, "We'll be sure to be praying for you as you carry on here."

Dr. Tozer answered, "Harry, is that 'piosity,' or do you really mean it?"

Harry Post

I was attending a meeting of district Christian education leaders sponsored by Mavis Weidman being held in Dr. Tozer's church. Mavis, anxious to seize the opportunity for input from such a great writer, asked Dr. Tozer to speak to us about how to be a good writer. I shall never forget his very pointed comments. "The only way to be a good writer is to have something worthwhile to write about. You can't write from an empty head."

Earl Swanson

In a visit to Tozer's church in Chicago his sense of humor came to the foreground. I was rather large at that time and overweight. He had insisted that I bring with me an Indian family and an Indian baby. I brought the family down from the Oneida Reservation in Wisconsin. Tozer, very much enamored with the baby, took the baby from the mother's arms, and taking it to the pulpit, showed the people. He brought it back to the mother and then proceeded to introduce me. When I got to the pulpit, I said, "You take notice that Dr. Tozer did not attempt to carry me to the pulpit." The place came apart and Tozer himself was bent double with laughter. The meeting was off to a good start.

Dr. Keith M. Bailey

After World War 2, Tozer was financially helping a German family through Project CARE. This was unbeknownst to just about everyone. Eventually the family was back on its feet again, and Project CARE asked him to consider sponsoring another family. But knowing that Tozer was a Protestant minister, they asked if it would be a problem that the family was Catholic. Tozer responded, "Why would that make a difference in helping someone?"

Stan Lemon

❧

At a special service in which a well-known pastor was featuring the hymnody of Dr. A.B. Simpson, I sat next to Dr. Tozer on the platform. As the program progressed, the pastor was deeply moved by the special rendition of Simpson's hymns. At one point he was overcome with emotion—so much so that he was unable to talk for a few moments. Dr. Tozer leaned over to me and said, "Something like this is all right once in five years."

Harry Post

❧

Tozer said he would only read a book until he came to the point where God spoke to him. Then he would close the book and listen to the words of God rather than the words of men. Apparently he didn't finish many books.

Stan Lemon

❧

Although Dr. Tozer's art form was language and literature, his interest ranged in other areas, especially music. During the last years of his life he became quite a lover of Bach and Beethoven, although I think he admired Beethoven more. (In fact, on one occasion he expressed his desire to have the "Missa Solemnis" performed at his funeral.) At home in the evenings he would often lie and listen to great music. I remember Ravel's "Bolero" was a particular favorite. He claimed it relaxed him, a statement that taxed my imagination!

Raymond McAfee

The entire focus of Dr. A.W. Tozer's preaching and writing was on God. He had no time for religious hucksters who were inventing new ways to promote their wares and inflate their statistics. Like Thoreau, whom he read and admired, Tozer marched to a different drummer; and for this reason, he was usually out of step with many of the people in the religious parade.

Warren W. Wiersbe

I remember an occasion which was typical of his quiet wisdom. I sat with him as we listened to a fellow minister give an eloquent and moving sermon. The speaker repeatedly referred to the fact that he was delivering great truth, eternal truth. After the message, Dr. Tozer and I were walking on the campgrounds and he offered this valuable advice. He said, "It is never necessary, young man, to tell people that you are delivering great truth. The truth speaks for itself.

True greatness will never be denied. Lincoln did not find it necessary to tell people that they should make a special note of the significance of the Gettysburg address." He also warned me against levity or any attempt to make the truth of God palatable. He was profoundly convinced that nothing was more majestic or immutable or amazing than the clear teaching of the Word of God. To me this was the great secret of the man's greatness, coupled with his ability to express it in such a beautiful and simple and forcible manner.

William F. Bryan

When Dr. Tozer would come to New York City for meetings of the Board of Managers, the three-day session involved eating with friends in the restaurants that flourish in the Times Square area. The waiter or waitress would always inquire, "Do you want this all on one check?" This, of course, was the usual thing in the New York "expense account" way of life that was developing even before the advent of the ubiquitous credit card.

In the case of Mr. Tozer and his friends, all were on the same modest per diem allowance. This part of the meal always elicited some crisp remark from Tozer to the effect that of course we wanted separate checks since we did not have a bookkeeper along to divide up the total, and besides, who can treat whom under such circumstances?

Robert Battles

Tozer loved to listen to men like Dr. Zwemer, Dr. Max Reich and many others. And he had received two or three honorary degrees himself. Around the church we started to call him "Doctor," but he replied, "I'm still an intern, still learning."

Everyone would smile over that.

J. Francis Chase

It must not be thought that his writings are from sermon tapes. Dr. Tozer would take his sermon notes as seeds for articles or books and carefully and painstakingly rework them into the literary form he wanted. It was his thesis that hard writing meant easy reading. He would sit in his study bent over his portable typewriter with a green eyeshade to protect his light-sensitive eyes, wearing a sweater with the elbows out, and pound out editorials and books with Webster's Unabridged Dictionary within easy reach.

Raymond McAfee

On the lighter side, Dr. Tozer despised power lawn mowers! After a meal in the dining hall at Beulah Beach, Dr. Tozer was standing on the balcony watching the hapless maintenance man mow the lawn with a power mower.

I happened to be the closest person to Dr. Tozer at the moment, so he turned to me and delivered a dissertation about power lawn mowers the likes of which I have never heard in my life. His command of the English language, even on this very practical issue, was overwhelming.

Earl M. Swanson

"He had a great appreciation for the elders, Sunday school teachers and other helpers. Certainly no pastor was more fulsome in open expressions of appreciation for the office-bearers of his church. He trusted them and leaned heavily upon them to carry the load of decision making, administration, and disciplining of the people."

Dr. Louis L. King
A.W. Tozer: An Anthology

8

Chicago

God sometimes places his people in specific geographical locations—and A.W. Tozer found his in Chicago. Although he did not know it as he headed his car westward from Indianapolis, Chicago would be his home for the next 31 years and the Southside Gospel Tabernacle, at 70th and Union, his major forum.

Chicago in 1928, with some 3.3 million people, was the world's fourth largest city, after New York, London and Berlin. It was second only to New York in aggregate wealth. In an era when dollars were valuable, the city boasted at least 100 millionaires, headed by names like Armour, Field, McCormick, Palmer, Pullman. These elite managed to secure wide-ranging city planning: lakefront parks, boulevards, forest preserves. Chicago was a manufacturing and transportation hub. More than a thousand trains a day entered and departed from its seven passenger terminals serving all of North America. Its banking, commerce and service industries dominated the entire Midwest. Only New York could be a fit comparison for its grandeur, wealth and power.

The many sides of Chicago

But there were the other sides of Chicago, too. Dwight L. Moody's Bible institute, with a galaxy of well-known professors such as Reuben A. Torrey and James M. Gray, was a lodestone for those serious about Christian evangelism. The related Moody Memorial Church had already been served by such well-known preachers as R.A. Torrey, Paul Rader, A.C. Dixon and P.W. Philpott with other luminaries, like H.A. Ironside, still to come. Wheaton College graduates would later spawn a plethora of evangelical ministries, many of them based in the greater Chicago area.

During the early years of the century Chicago had seen a massive influx of migrants: Germans, Poles, Bohemians, Slovaks, Irish, Lithuanians, Ukrainians and peoples from a dozen other European nations. Most were males, lured by wages far beyond anything they could expect at home. Some scrimped to save as much as $500 so they could return to their homelands to live in luxury off their American wealth. Others sent for their families as soon as they could.

Those who stayed became the stable working class of the 1920s and 30s. World War 1 had ended the massive immigration; by 1929, the pool of unskilled labor was shrinking drastically. Meanwhile, land values had escalated as the city expanded westward.

Prohibition in America had created a new, incredibly profitable industry that rewarded those willing to be forceful and ruthless. Chicago was Exhibit A of the seamier side of this illicit enterprise. The city gained a reputation as the world's crime capital, with Al Capone its prime minister. Political bosses like Mayor "Big Bill" Thompson gave the word corruption new dimensions. Gang wars, in the space of half a decade, 1926–30, killed some 200 victims. Racketeering and labor violence were only slightly less spectacular.

"Chicago . . . forever keeps two faces," wrote Nelson Ahlgren in his classic *Chicago: City on the Make,* "one for winners and one for losers, one for hustlers and one for squares. . . . One face for Go-Getters and one for Go-Get-It-Yourselfers." Studs Terkel, celebrated Chicago poet, summed up the city succinctly: "Chicago is America's dream, writ large. And flamboyantly."

Such was the Chicago of 1928 that greeted Tozer and his family as the faithful 1925 Oakland carried them through the southeastern industrial suburbs to their destination on the south side.

It did not take long for word of Tozer's ministry to

spread throughout the substantial evangelical community of the city. Tozer attracted people who wanted their minds stimulated as well as their souls. An excellent system of public transportation made the church easily accessible, and people began traveling from near and far to hear this remarkable preacher. Professors in the evangelical schools were drawn to him and recommended him to their students. Some of those new people who occupied the pews Sunday afternoon and evening were members of mainline churches dissatisfied with the Bibleless preaching from their own pulpits and hungry for the solid meat of God's Word.

Steady growth

Southside Gospel Tabernacle grew, not explosively but steadily, and so did the stature of its young pastor. Many attended the nearby Dutch Reformed Church in the morning and then went to Tozer's church in the afternoon and evening. At the time the church's services were 2:00 p.m. for Sunday School, 3:00 p.m. for the worship service and 7:30 p.m. for the evangelistic service.

Tozer's vision for the Chicago church was that it be a place to which people came expecting God to be present. The Holy Spirit was prevalent at the church; as one member reflected, "You could feel it when you walked in."

Students who heard Tozer at Southside Gospel Tabernacle invited him to speak at their meetings. He relished these encounters and seldom turned one down. His influence upon the students was considerable. They loved him and he loved them. Biographer David J. Fant wrote, "Young people by the score responded to the call for Christian service and now may be found in churches and missions in many parts of the world."

Tozer's preaching attracted good men to the congregation who provided leadership and actually carried much of the administrative responsibility in the church, freeing Tozer to concentrate on the church's spiritual ministry. Under capable leaders, the Sunday school grew to around 500 members, reaching into the church's neighborhood. Church women met all day every Wednesday to keep updated on overseas missionary activity and to pray for the international work of The Christian and Missionary Alliance.

The church gained a reputation for its excellent music. Tozer was not himself musical, but he had a deep appreciation for the solid hymnody of the church. Men such as J. Stratton Shufelt and Raymond McAfee, who served for 15 years as Tozer's minister of music at Southside Gospel Tabernacle, contributed inestimably to the church's impact on the weekly worshipers. Several of the church's Easter musicales were featured on national radio.

During the 1930s, Southside Gospel Tabernacle slowly developed from a loosely-structured parachurch into a well-machined, full-fledged church. Its focus on missions and the deeper life in Christ Jesus did not change; its organization did. And in keeping with the organizational changes, Southside Gospel Tabernacle became Southside Alliance Church. By then physical expansion was overdue. At each service the sanctuary was at capacity and beyond.

Next to the church was an old dilapidated building. The plan was to buy the building, tear it down and build a new sanctuary in its place, retaining the existing church structure for Christian education purposes. Many within the congregation were skeptical about the project. To them it seemed like a massive undertaking. But the majority was in favor of the plan and gave a green light to the building committee. A bond issue was soon subscribed by the congregation, and money was in hand.

J. Francis Chase, a member of the congregation and chairman of the church board, helped design the new facility. The ensuing half century has seen remarkable refinements in church building appointments. Today it is amusing to think that an *Alliance Life* reporter would gush about "linotile"-covered floors in the new Chicago sanctuary, or about "linowall" wall covering to the window sills. But when it was completed in 1941, just prior to America's entry into World War 2, the "light gray brick" Chicago church was "modern in construction and attractive in appearance, both without and within."

The sanctuary could accommodate 800 people, including a balcony and an 80-chair choir loft. No expense was spared in its design and construction. Recessed ceiling fixtures diffused light evenly over the auditorium. Instead of oak pews, upholstered opera seats provided living-room comfort for the worshipers. In deference to Chicago summers, the building was cooled on the hottest days by circulating air blown over huge blocks of ice through the heating ducts. An innovation at the time—which would be generously copied—was a glass-fronted mother's room at the back of the auditorium where those with small children could participate in the service without the risk that their crying offspring might distract other worshipers.

Additional classrooms in the full basement, all completely furnished, together with the old sanctuary, expanded the Sunday school's capacity to some 1,200 students.

Ahead of its time

It was a building ahead of its time. For years church committees journeyed to Chicago to tour the facility and borrow ideas for their own building projects. It was the talk of the community. During the building program the missions giving soared to an all-time high and maintained that level.

In a city with more than its share of Bible-believing, Bible-teaching churches, Southside Alliance was regarded by many as the citadel of fundamental churches. Tozer was proud of both the new building and the church's reputation.

An entire week was set aside to dedicate the new facility. Tozer invited leaders from The Christian and Missionary Alliance as well as church dignitaries in the Chicago community for the celebration. He was anxious to show off the new building.

Finally, dedication week was over. The important leaders had unanimously congratulated Tozer on a job well done and had wished him God's blessing for the future. It was Monday morning, and Tozer was in his small study at the top of the steps behind the platform. He was reflecting on the week just past. It gave him a good feeling. The Pennsylvania farm boy had made it big in America's second largest city. The years of hard work were finally paying off.

Suddenly, his heart was smitten with conviction. Only once—in one of his books—did he divulge the essence of that Monday morning session with God. God dealt with his heart, and He was not too gentle, either. Tozer would only say that after that experience with God, he quietly went around to each room in the new building and gave it all back to God. It was no longer Tozer's building. Another idol had been torn from his heart. He would leave Chicago whenever God wanted him to.

During the next few years, Tozer's reputation and ministry enjoyed a steady increase. Many invited him to their conference platforms, their summer Bible camps, their Christian gatherings of all descriptions. People came to his study for counsel. People like the young evangelist, Billy Graham. People like politician Mark O. Hatfield. They sought out Tozer because they knew he was a man well acquainted with God.

War weighs heavily

The war years were a heavy burden on Tozer. He saw many of the young men of his congregation go off to war, including his own oldest son, Lowell. Often he would rise at 4:30 in the morning to have breakfast with one or more of these young men of his church and to walk them to the streetcar, where he would see them off. He interceded with God for their well-being, and he suffered when any of them suffered.

"His face was drawn and ashen white," Francis Chase said of Tozer, recalling those days. "I would stop by often and we would pray together, especially when he learned that Lowell was somewhere in the Italian campaign."

Three of Tozer's six sons were in military service during the war and two were wounded in combat.

Lowell was an enlisted man in an Army tank-destroyer unit and fought with them through North Africa, the landing at Salerno, and northward in Italy to the crossing of the Rapido River where he was wounded in one of the most furious and controversial battles of the war.

Forrest, known as Bud, the second oldest, served in the Marine Corps through the war, all in the United States. In 1946 he was released to reserve status. In 1950 he was recalled to active duty. Bud was wounded on December 6, 1950, while leading his marine platoon in the breakout of the First Marine Division from encirclement by about 15 Chinese divisions at the Chosin reservoir.

The Korean conflict was a continuation of the ordeal, both for the nation and for A.W. Tozer. Bud was a marine lieutenant when the Chinese swarmed across the Yalu River, forcing the American troops into disorganized retreat. "Those were heavy days," Chase continued. "Forrest was in that conflict. Shells were bursting all around our troops, and some shrapnel tore Bud's leg and knee tremendously. He was lying at the side of the road in subzero weather. A tank rumbled by with some boys huddled together on top of it, and one of them happened to glance down and saw Bud.

" 'Lieutenant,' he yelled, 'what are you doing down there?'

" 'I can't walk,' Bud yelled back. So they stopped and lifted him onto the tank. How painful that rough ride must have been. Tozer was delighted to discover that his boy wasn't killed and that there was prospect of saving his leg. Bud has limped from that day to this, but he is still here!"

"I arrived," Bud remembered, "at Great Lakes Naval Hospital, 40 miles north of Chicago, on Christmas night, 1950, just 19 days after being wounded. My parents visited me the next day and brought me three books—a large type Bible, King James Version of course, and the two small volumes of radio talks by C. S. Lewis, later combined to make up the classic, *Mere Christianity.*"

Aiden, Jr., third oldest son, served throughout World War 2 in the Navy Air Corps and was a Gunner's Mate 1st Class, flying as rear gunner in a torpedo bomber from a Jeep carrier when he was wounded by Japanese antiaircraft fire somewhere in the Pacific.

Wendell, the fourth oldest, served in the Navy and Raleigh, fifth oldest, was in the Marine Corps, but neither for long and neither in combat.

Peace or war or peace again, Tozer never departed from a regular pulpit ministry of feeding his flock.

Once he encountered a man who did not believe in going to church each week to hear the Word of God preached. The man felt that once people were converted, they should immediately turn their full attention to winning others. "A farmer," the man argued, "candles his eggs once, not every week. As soon as the eggs have been candled, he crates them and ships them off to market."

Tozer found a serious flaw in the man's argument. "Christ did not say to Peter, 'Candle my eggs.' He said, 'Feed my sheep.' Christians are not eggs to be candled but sheep to be fed. Feeding sheep is not something you do once for all. It is a loving act you repeat regularly as long as the sheep live."

In that sense, Tozer was a faithful shepherd of the flock of God. In his 31 years of Chicago ministry his sermons covered every phase of Christian life. He preached on the great doctrines of justification and sanctification, on the attributes of God, on worship. Frequently, he preached through books of both the Old and New Testament. He was never bound by times and seasons. Always his preaching was practical and related to the spiritual needs of people.

Tozer's reputation in the city was further enhanced when WMBI, the Moody Bible Institute radio station, asked him to fill a Saturday morning slot vacated by Wilbur M. Smith, who had accepted a teaching position on the West Coast. "Talks from a Pastor's Study" actually originated in Tozer's church study. There he would stand—never sit—and deliver his message as if a congregation was in front of him. Many area preachers listened regularly and expressed their appreciation. The station rated it one of their most popular programs.

Chicago shaped Tozer and his ministry, and he in turn shaped at least the evangelical side of Chicago. Despite its flagrant faults, he loved the city. "Everywhere I put my finger in this city," he once remarked, "I can feel a pulse." Tozer may have been willing to leave Chicago should the Lord so direct, but his personal preference was clear. And his amply-fed congregation was certainly content to let things remain that way.

TOZER-GRAMS

It is possible within the provisions of redemptive grace to enter into a state of union with Christ so perfect that the world will instinctively react toward us exactly as it did toward Him in the days of His flesh.

It is the Spirit of Christ in us that will draw Satan's fire. The people of the world will not much care what we believe, and they will stare vacantly at our religious forms, but there is one thing they will never forgive us, the presence of God's Spirit in our hearts.

A world of confusion and disappointment results from trying to believe without obeying. This puts us in the position of a bird trying to fly with one wing folded. We merely flap in a circle and seek to cheer our hearts with the hope that the whirling ball of feathers is proof that a revival is under way.

Many a splendid church has drifted into modernism because its leaders would not insist on the everlasting importance of the basic doctrines of the faith; and many a church split has resulted from an undue attachment to nonessentials.

Contending for the faith once delivered to the saints may not always mean fighting to retain the major tenets of the Christian creed. It can mean, as well, striving to maintain a proper balance between all the doctrines of the faith in their relation to each other and to the whole.

Overstress the minors, and you have chaos; overlook the majors, and you have death.

PRAYER

Lord, how great is our dilemma! In Thy Presence silence best becomes us, but love inflames our hearts and constrains us to speak.

Were we to hold our peace the stones would cry out; yet if we speak, what shall we say? Teach us to know that we cannot know, for the things of God knoweth no man, but the Spirit of God. Let faith support us where reason fails, and we shall think because we believe, not in order that we may believe.

In Jesus' name. Amen.

"God Incomprehensible"
The Knowledge of the Holy

"Largely self-taught, Dr. Tozer knew language like few others. He was a precise craftsman in its use. But those who pressed to hear him preach, including great numbers of college and university students, found in A.W. Tozer more than a master wordsmith. They saw in him a man to whom the knowledge of God and Christian experience were supreme realities."

Robert W. Battles
Men Who Met God

9

Preacher

Primarily, A.W. Tozer was a preacher. All else revolved around his pulpit ministry. His writing, for example, was simply an extension of his preaching. His pursuit of God found appropriate expression in his preaching and his writing.

During the 1930s and 40s, Tozer's preaching gained attention in the Chicago area because it was different. While others were offering clever outlines and meticulous word studies, Tozer led his listeners straight into the presence of God. That was his goal, his objective in preaching.

He studiously avoided any artificiality in his preaching. Alliteration he regarded as in that category and avoided it. Anything that might distract from the core message or block his hearers' path to God was ruthlessly cut out. His sermons were warm and alive, like flowers opening under the glowing rays of the sun to let their fragrances be enjoyed by the beholders. He worked hard not to sound like a typical preacher. He did not want his sermons to sound like sermons, so he structured them more like magazine articles, teaching spiritual principles rather than reciting the exegesis of verses.

There was an aura of saintliness about the man. Saintliness and authority. When he walked to the pulpit to preach, the audience sensed that, like Aaron, the high priest of Israel, he had first appeared before God to intercede for his people. Like Aaron, he was now ready to pronounce a benediction upon them. However, his father once commented on his preaching, "You look like you're always falling down or getting up."

Tozer spent hours in sermon preparation. He preached from an outline carefully handwritten on both inside halves of a folded sheet of 8" x 10" paper, which he clipped to the pages of his Bible. The major part of his preparation was prayer. His sermons were steeped in prayer; they were a declaration of what he had discovered in prayer.

Tozer believed that certain neglected truths must be stressed: world missions, prophecy, divine healing, separation from worldly things, the work of the Holy Spirit, heart purity, personal victory over self and sin, the indwelling Christ, the importance of worship. There must be courageous adherence to the New Testament pattern.

Distinct style

In preaching Tozer held his Bible in his left hand and with his right hand followed his notes. Probably no person heard Tozer preach more often or in more diverse situations than Ray McAfee, Tozer's longtime associate. During those years Tozer did not own a car, so McAfee drove him to his numerous speaking appointments in the area. No sooner were the two men in the car than Tozer would begin reading from Watts, Wesley, Fenelon, Faber. He would read a few lines, place the book across his knees and begin to comment. Together the two critically examined almost every Shakespearean plot, the sentimental charm of Burns' "Tam O'Shanter," the sublime nature poetry of Wordsworth and the magnificence of Milton's noble works, from which Tozer quoted frequently in his addresses. "Tozer polished his spirit in worship, and his mind in great literature and philosophy," McAfee said.

"His preaching," McAfee adds, "was like the action of an eagle. For the first five minutes it was the eagle pulling its head out from under its wings, looking around and blinking. Then for a few minutes the bird stretched its wings and shook its tail. Finally, after 10 minutes or so, it took off and began to soar.

"Tozer often stood on his toes when he preached. He rarely moved from behind the pulpit. He never was demonstrative. He spoke in a quiet voice and learned how to emphasize things by snapping the sentence with a word."

There were times in his preaching when he would lay his Bible on the pulpit. "I learned," McAfee reflected, "to pay especially close attention at those times. It was a sign that Tozer was seeing something while preaching that he had not seen in his preparation." James M. Gray once remarked that in his lifetime he knew very few people who could think on their feet while they were preaching, and one was A.W. Tozer.

Listeners to Tozer's preaching frequently had the feeling that he was turning on a water faucet and then turning it off when there was enough. He would begin by reading his text, usually brief, and then he would say, "Now, I want to make a few remarks by way of introduction." Then, without the listener realizing how much time had slipped by, he would say, "Well, I see my time is up. I'll stop here and finish this tonight."

Tozer never seemed to be hurried in his preaching. He refused to be under bondage to times and seasons. He followed the cloud, not the calendar. Once he took three years to work his way through the Gospel of John, one of his favorite Bible books. His congregation found it neither tiresome nor repetitious. They were hearing old truths declared boldly and in fresh, sparkling, sometimes startling expressions.

Sermon preparation was a constant process with

Tozer. It did not matter if he was riding a streetcar or train or if someone was driving him to an appointment across town. He would get settled in his seat and immediately out would come a book. It might be a book he was reading at the time, or a spiral notebook in which he would jot down sermon notes. He was constantly reading and studying and thinking and writing.

At times, Tozer might have sermon outlines prepared two or three weeks in advance. There were other times when inspiration did not come easily. He could spend hours mulling over a word or a phrase. "Get the idea clear," he used to say, "and the words will take care of themselves during delivery."

Tozer's sermons were never shallow. There was hard thinking behind them, and Tozer forced his hearers to think with him. He had the ability to make his listeners face themselves in the light of what God was saying to them. The flippant did not like Tozer; the serious who wanted to know what God was saying to them loved him. Often his messages were so strong—and long—some wished he would stop and let them catch their breath.

Study with a purpose

As a rule, as in his sermons on the Gospel of John, Tozer assigned himself a chapter or a Bible book or a theme for his preaching schedule. He felt that it helped him to keep on track in his preparation. He emphasized that a preacher should study for a purpose and read with a purpose.

Over the years his appetite for, and acquisition of, books increased. On his speaking engagements in other major cities, he frequently could be found rummaging through the offerings of a secondhand bookstore. He loved the unusual, and his library held books unknown to the average reader. He read theology, history, philosophy, poetry and literature in general. He was especially attracted to the ancient writers, particularly the church fathers and Christian mystics.

High above all other books was the Bible, which he read diligently. He possessed 40 different versions. With dictionary, lexicon and concordance at hand, he sought the etymology of all doubtful words. He devoted long hours to the memorization of the Scriptures. The accuracy and appropriateness of his quotations testify to his familiarity with the Bible.

Tozer early realized that to be effective in preaching, he would have to develop sensitivity and precision in the use of words. He developed an aversion to what he called "dead words" and led a vigorous crusade against clichés. After becoming editor of *Alliance Life*, he issued an "Index Prohibitorum" of words and phrases he considered overworked or spent and no longer worthy of use. He insisted that these be excised from any manuscript accepted for publication.

Tozer's speaking voice was not particularly strong, and there was a distinct nasal quality about it. He soon decided that he needed to do something about this deficit. Typical of Tozer, he went to a bookstore and purchased a volume on voice training to learn all he could about voice control. In his office was a large copy of Milton's *Paradise Lost.* Tozer would place it on a music stand borrowed from the sanctuary and read it aloud. He read through the book at least four times in order to strengthen his voice and gain better control of it.

To strengthen his lungs, Tozer would blow up balloons. In his briefcase he carried a supply of balloons for this purpose. Vanity? No. Simply an effort to be his best in God's service.

Planned worship

The worship service was Tozer's special concern. Every part of the order had to be planned and prayed over ahead of time. He despised spur-of-the-moment services pieced together without preparation. "A prayerfully planned order of service," he once said, "is not incompatible with the most joyful freedom in worship and possesses the advantage that it commands respect and avoids criticism."

Incongruously, he had one exception to his insistence on a planned order of service. He never selected the final hymn ahead of time. Tozer wanted that to be prompted by the Holy Spirit at the last moment. During his years at Southside, McAfee had the responsibility of selecting the final hymn while Tozer was preaching. Toward the end of McAfee's ministry in Chicago, Tozer confessed to him that he had played a little game. "After I finished preaching I would sit down and say to myself, 'I wonder what hymn he has chosen this time.' And so many times you chose what I thought you would choose."

In his preaching Tozer exercised great control. He refused to permit his enthusiasm for his subject to overpower his mind. His audience, while sensing the divine anointing on his preaching, sensed also that the spirit of the prophet was subject to the control of the prophet.

Tozer's illustrations could be grotesque, as when he likened reading a new Bible translation with optional alternate renderings to "shaving with a banana." But invariably he got his point across. Listeners knew what he meant. Even in private conversation he spoke figuratively, due, no doubt, to his training and reading.

Tozer's preaching was pointed and incisive. Listeners sensed that he was dealing with life principles that he was calling each auditor to discipleship and to the reality of God. His messages were not calculated to attract the frivolous and the shallow—and they did not. People either came to terms with God or they stopped attending because they found the scalpel uncomfortably sharp. At no time did his Sunday morning congregation in Chicago average more than 400–500 people.

Seldom did Tozer issue an "altar call" at the conclusion of a sermon. Not that he particularly objected to it, but it was not in his disposition. In fact, he regarded large responses with some skepticism. Occasionally on a Sunday evening he might announce, "There's a room over here to my right, and some of the brethren will put the lights on and receive you if you wish to come to pray." That was all.

After one powerful Sunday evening message Tozer

told the congregation, "It would be easy for me to have the altar filled, but I'm afraid I would do it in the flesh. I'm going to ask you not to talk as you leave the service and just go home. Go to your bedrooms, go to your living rooms, get the passage of Scripture out and say, 'God, what are you saying to me?' "

But the absence of large numbers "coming forward" did not mean the Spirit of God was not working. On a number of occasions, after Tozer returned home from church, someone would telephone him to announce that he or she had come to terms with Christ as a result of his message. That was the sort of deliberate, unemotional commitment Tozer was looking for. His concern was that people come to terms with Christ. Conversions took place routinely at the Chicago church.

Conference speaker

As a conference speaker, Tozer was in demand from many different denominations. It was a formidable schedule that he maintained for years, and people wondered how he could do it. Like all itinerant preachers, he had his "traveling sermons." In his conference ministry, Tozer would usually preach those sermons that had been especially blessed of God in his own pulpit.

Once at a conference Tozer was dining with Louis King, whose wife, Esther, had grown up in Southside Alliance. Tozer turned to Esther and asked, "Have you heard my sermon on 'A Hoary Head Is a Crown of Glory'?"

"Yes, I have," Mrs. King replied. "But why do you ask?"

"Well," Tozer responded thoughtfully, "do you think that it would be a good sermon for tonight?"

"I believe it would be."

"I've preached that sermon 32 times already," Tozer continued, "and tonight will make it 33." That night he preached the sermon for the 33rd time with profound effect upon the conference congregation.

Tozer could be hard-hitting if he felt the occasion demanded it. Invited by a holiness church to speak at the dedication of a new sanctuary, he suffered through a lengthy program of what he considered inappropriate levity topped by a women's trio who sang a selection of popular secular songs. When it came his turn to speak, he scrapped his prepared sermon.

"What is the matter with you holiness people?" Tozer began. "You used to have standards, but now the only way to tell that you are Christians is if you tell us." And, as only Tozer could, he took that entire assembled congregation to the spiritual woodshed for an unforgettable chastening.

Protocol was the farthest thing from Tozer's mind. He never preached to be invited back. He once remarked to D. Martin Lloyd-Jones, the noted London minister, that he had preached himself off every major Bible conference in the country. His concern was not to build a favorable personal reputation. Rather, his concern was to exalt Jesus Christ and to speak on behalf of God. The chips could fall where they would.

At the same time, Tozer never publicly attacked individuals or churches that might have strayed from the truth. "If a denomination does something that we object to and we attack it, we shall have a little war on our hands. If we deal with its wrongs in a broader way, we correct the abuse and warn others against it without naming those involved. When you lay down spiritual rules and deep-lying principles and show that they are violated in current Christianity, you can trust intelligent people to make their own applications."

There were times when a young ministerial student would get the opportunity to spend some time in Tozer's study. Mostly it would be a young man from the congregation. One student who happened to visit with Tozer finally got around to asking him about his filing system.

"Are you really interested in that?" Tozer asked.

When the student replied affirmatively, Tozer pulled out a bottom desk drawer, showed him a pile of papers and said, "That's it!"

Frequently Tozer had opportunity to address theology students on the subject of preaching. It was something he delighted in. To him, preaching was the most important thing a minister did. He observed that, historically, preaching has drawn the multitudes to Christ.

Preaching begins with prayer

"True preaching always begins in prayer," Tozer would tell the students. "Any sermon that does not originate in prayer is not a message from God no matter how learned the speaker. It does no good to make up sermons to preach. Preaching must be the present voice of God to a particular people."

Tozer never gloried in his lack of formal education. "I believe," he insisted, "a preacher must be as educated as he possibly can be."

He likened the preacher to an artist. "An artist works in watercolors, oils, sandstone, gold, glass, marble. The preacher, on the other hand, works in the stuff called mankind. The artist has an idea of abstract beauty and he seeks to reproduce it in visible, concrete things. The preacher has Christ and tries to make Him visible in human lives. The artist has genius; the preacher has the Holy Spirit. The artist draws his inspiration from other artists; the preacher draws his inspiration in prayer alone with God. The artist's tools are brushes, chisels, flame. The tools of the preacher are words. Like the artist, a preacher must master his tools. At first he will make awkward attempts, but if he keeps at it, he will become an expert."

Every preacher, Tozer believed, must develop the habit of judicious reading.

"Never read a 'good book,' " he cautioned. "There are many good books being published every year. The majority of them merely rehash what someone else has written. Go back to the classics and learn from them. Read some of the great Puritan authors and some of the mystics. Read and memorize good poetry. Observe how these writers express themselves."

To develop verbal skill, Tozer offered these masters for study: John Bunyan for simplicity; Joseph Addison for clarity and elegance; John Milton for nobility and consistent elevation of thought; Charles Dickens for sprightliness ("start with *A Christmas Carol*"); Francis Bacon for conciseness and dignity. In addition, Tozer recommended Robert Louis Stevenson, John Ruskin, Thomas Carlyle, Nathaniel Hawthorne and the poetry of Wordsworth, Bryant, Blake, Keats and Shelley.

"Become word conscious," he would exhort. "Pay attention to words and the effect they have. Get and use a good dictionary. If you come across an unfamiliar word, look it up immediately and study it. In that way you are building your vocabulary all the time. Some would have you believe that a large vocabulary will cause you to speak over the heads of people. Actually, the opposite is the case. With a large vocabulary you are able to be precise in what you say. Nothing takes the place of using the right word." One of the trademarks of Tozer's preaching was his ability to have the right word always at his command.

Communication the key

One time while Tozer was having lunch with his son Wendell, the son confessed that he was having trouble understanding some mainline preachers because they seemed vague and abstract. Tozer's imagination took over. "The first thing," Tozer began, expounding on their seminary training, "freshmen are required to do is make a list of every concrete word in their vocabulary. Their second assignment is to learn several empty concepts or platitudes that can't possibly offend anyone. Assignment three, they are never to use those concrete words they had listed." Tozer then suggested that seminary students should be required to sell potato peelers at Woolworth's until they learned how to communicate.

TOZER-GRAMS

People, not ideas, should get first attention from the preacher. Yet we find many talented men who are cold toward people but fervent in their love for ideas. Terrible as it may be, it is yet true that one may spend a lifetime propagating religious ideas with little or no love for men back of it all.

Plain speech is to be admired, but a lot that passes for plain is simply rude. The trouble with the man who boasts that he calls a spade a spade is that he often ends by calling everything a spade. He sneers at every tender emotion, brands with the name of spade every simple human joy, and is buried at last with a spade—the latter office being perhaps the kindest one that humble implement ever performed for him. May God keep fresh the fountain of our laughter and our tears!

Many preachers have occasion to be thankful for the Revised Version margin. It is verily a present help in time of trouble. But I am always suspicious of any sermon that has to use crutches. If there is not plain Scripture enough to support the idea, better throw it out; it probably is not so anyway.

Every hope for the human race is based upon the

assumption that the nature of man can be changed from what it is to what it ought to be. Were the character of the individual static, all hope for the world would perish instantly.

Am I mistaken, or have I noticed among our churches a drift toward the observation of holy days and new moons and seasons? If such a thing is true, let us revolt against it. Let us throw off the yoke of bondage from which we were, at such great cost, set free.

PRAYER

It is a good thing to give thanks unto Thee and to sing praises unto Thy name, O Most High, to show forth Thy loving-kindness in the morning and Thy faithfulness every night. As Thy Son while on earth was loyal to Thee, His Heavenly Father, so now in heaven He is faithful to us, His earthly brethren; and in this knowledge we press on with every confident hope for all the years and centuries yet to come. Amen.

"The Faithfulness of God"
The Knowledge of the Holy

"That agile mind seemed always at work. In the inside pocket of his jacket he carried a ten-cent-store spiral notebook and several ballpoint pens. Wherever he was, he would jot down thoughts and ideas. He was usually in the midst of writing an editorial for the *Alliance Witness*, working on a book or preparing a sermon."

Raymond McAfee
Signposts

10

Writer

People invariably are surprised to learn that A.W. Tozer authored nine books. Those whose acquaintance with Tozer is limited to the bestselling *The Pursuit of God* are delighted to know he wrote other books still in print and available to them. Others, aware of the long list of nearly 40 Tozer titles in the annual catalog of Christian Publications, exclaim in disbelief, "Only nine?"

In his lifetime, Tozer wrote nine books:

Wingspread (1943), the biography of Albert B.

Simpson, founder of The Christian and Missionary Alliance, Tozer's church denomination.

Let My People Go (1947), the life story of a celebrated missionary, Robert A. Jaffray, who pioneered the Alliance work in Indochina and Indonesia and perished in the closing days of World War 2 in a Japanese concentration camp.

The Pursuit of God (1948), Tozer's first and best-known spiritual treatise. Translated into major foreign languages, its popularity continues to build.

The Divine Conquest (1950), Tozer's challenge to let the Holy Spirit cross the threshold of personality and inspire the soul.

The Root of the Righteous (1955), a collection of some of Tozer's earlier *Alliance Life* editorials, compiled and reedited by the author.

Keys to the Deeper Life (1957), a series of articles that Tozer wrote for a leading Christian magazine and later compiled in book form.

Born after Midnight (1959), a second collection of Tozer's *Alliance Life* editorials, compiled and reedited by the author.

Of God and Men (1960), the third and final collection of editorials compiled and reedited by the author.

The Knowledge of the Holy (1961), a study of the attributes of God. Some consider it his crowning literary achievement.

In addition to the above list, Tozer compiled *The Christian Book of Mystical Verse* (1963). As the title implies, it is a collection of poetry from the saintly mystics Tozer discovered in his insatiable search through history for spirits kindred to his own.

The other nearly 30 books have been assembled from Tozer's editorials not previously published in book form, or from tape recordings of his sermons fortuitously made and preserved by people of his Chicago and Toronto congregations.

Writing and preaching different

In his lifetime Tozer never allowed his recorded messages to be published. "You don't," he explained, "write the way you talk."

An officer of what is now Harper & Row pursued Tozer for years to obtain permission to reprint in book form a collection of his editorials from the *Alliance Life.* Tozer refused on the grounds that he did not have time to rewrite them. The Harper & Row man told him they did not want him to change a word. Tozer's answer was still no, because, in Tozer's judgment, the editorials he had written before were amateurish and not up to the standards he expected of himself.

Actually, Tozer's first foray into the field of writing, apart from the Indianapolis church newspaper, was through the medium of *Alliance Life.* Together with a number of articles submitted to and published in that denominational magazine, Tozer wrote two short, chatty columns, "A Word in Season" and "There's Truth in It," carried by the magazine during the 1930s and 40s. His byline could be found in other evangelical magazines as well.

Writing, and especially writing a book, was not something Tozer took lightly. "The only book that should ever be written is one that flows up from the heart, forced out by the inward pressure," he often cautioned aspiring writers. "You should never write a book unless you just have to." Throughout his ministry, he followed his own advice. Many editors called upon him for articles and books, but he rarely responded to their appeals.

Attack on Christian writers

Once he was invited to speak at an annual conference of Christian writers in Chicago. The director was introduced to Dr. Tozer and began to explain to him the reason for the conference. "Our purpose here, Dr. Tozer, is to encourage beginning writers to perfect their technique." In an absent sort of way Dr. Tozer nodded affirmatively.

The director of the conference was acquainted with Tozer but only by reputation and was completely unprepared for what happened. Much to the director's horror, Tozer proceeded to tear apart in no uncertain terms the idea that Christian fiction was a legitimate means of spreading the gospel of Jesus Christ. It was a blistering attack on Christian writers who used fiction to communicate the truths of Jesus Christ.

He began his presentation by confessing that his was a minority report and that he must disagree with good friends. He then proceeded to talk about "The Cult of Imitation," "The Cult of Entertainment" and "The Cult of the Celebrity." His charges were that Christian writers of the day no longer innovated but rather were too involved in imitating the world. He pointed out what he called a destructive heresy that religion is a form of entertainment. "This has given us," Tozer said, "a type of religious fiction that is unrealistic, affected and false." He was also totally against the idea that a work of literature could be built around the converted celebrity. To emphasize his point he quoted from St. Ignatius, "Apart from [Christ] let nothing dazzle you."

The summation of his talk was that fiction was false, a perpetrator of error and hence totally beneath the high art of Christian writing.

After Dr. Tozer was finished the director tried to pick up the pieces and smooth over, at least a little, what Tozer had said. The director was completely exasperated.

None of Tozer's books were written to establish his reputation or for monetary reward. Rather, his books sprang from a deeply burdened heart. He had a message from God that had to be conveyed. In his preface to *The Divine Conquest*, he explains, "The sight of the languishing church around me and the operation of a new spiritual power within me have set up a pressure impossible to resist. Whether or not the book ever reaches a wide public, still it has to be written if for no other reason than to relieve an unbearable burden on the heart."

That sequence applied to all his books. In prayer, Tozer discovered that God was entrusting him with a particular message—what the biblical prophets called a "burden." In time that burden would be the theme of a series of sermons preached to his church congregation. Away from his own pulpit, he would preach those same sermons to diverse audiences. If the burden intensified, weighing him down to the point of no release, he knew it was time to take pen in hand. The fruit of his writing eventuated in a book.

Writing the classic

Tozer was struggling under the increasing pressure of the first of these burdens when he received an invitation to preach in McAllen, Texas—far down toward the Mexican border. He saw in it an opportunity. The long train ride from Chicago would afford him ample time to think and to write.

As he boarded the Pullman at the old LaSalle Street Station, Tozer requested of the porter a small writing table for his roomette. There, with only his Bible before him, he began to write. About 9:00 p.m. the porter knocked on the door. "This is the last call for dinner," he announced. "Would you want me to bring you something to eat?"

"Yes," Tozer responded. "Please bring me some toast and tea." With only toast and tea to fortify him physically, Tozer continued to write. He wrote all night long, the words coming to him as fast as he could jot them down. The manuscript was almost writing itself, so full of his subject was he. Early the next morning when the train pulled into McAllen, a rough draft of *The Pursuit of God* was complete.

The main thesis of *The Pursuit of God* is achieving the heart's true goal in God. Although Tozer approached his subject from various angles, he never departed from his central theme—God and man's relation to Him, and how to maintain that relationship. One reviewer said, "The style is natural, free and easy, abounding in the pithy sentences that characterize Tozer's writing. In some of the chapters the movement is more stately, the tone rather philosophical. It awakens thought and expectancy, and while never heavy it is profound."

The Pursuit of God catapulted Tozer into the forefront of what was still in 1948 a relatively small group of evangelical writers. Readers rushed out to buy copies. Here was a penetrating message for the 20th century, written in a style refreshingly different.

The book's success was a pleasant surprise for Tozer. In reply to an especially appreciative letter, Tozer wrote: "After reading your letter I am left with few words. I am both gratified and awestruck. 'This is the Lord's doing; it is marvelous in our eyes.' The blessing that has rested on this little book is so much greater than I had dared to hope that I cannot say God is blessing it because of my prayers."

Probably the fact that his writings were born of such soul struggle explains their wide circulation and continued usefulness. *The Pursuit of God* has been translated into Arabic, Armenian, Chinese, Dutch, German, Greek, Gujarati (India), Hindi (India), Japanese, Kisukuma (Tanzania), Korean, Marathi (India), Portuguese, Romanian and Spanish. No methodical count has been maintained, but circulation of the English edition alone has easily passed the million mark.

Tozer labored over everything he wrote. "Hard writing makes for easy reading," he often said. He worked and struggled until each sentence was exactly the way he wanted it. He read aloud every line to check for repetition or imprecision. His style was lean, precise, often cryptic.

Many people who visited Tozer in his second-floor study behind the platform of Southside Alliance Church were surprised at the smallness of the book-lined room. In the center was his desk, on which were the volumes he referred to frequently. He wanted them close at hand, especially his Unabridged Webster's Dictionary within easy reach at his side and always open. A gooseneck lamp on the desk offered illumination.

Tozer, dressed in a business suit, rode in a noisy, dirty, uncomfortable streetcar the five miles from home to his church office. Once in the office, to preserve the crease in his suit trousers, he would exchange them for a decrepit garment he called his "praying pants." He wore tinted, rimless glasses, and when he was at his desk he shaded his eyes with a green visor of the kind popularized by newspapermen in that era. He worked in a vest. Rubber bands at his elbows kept his shirt cuffs from getting in the way. Out of that small study came sermons, books, magazine editorials and articles that have been a blessing to hundreds of thousands of people.

Nothing superficial, obvious or trivial

In his writing Tozer left the superficial, the obvious and the trivial for others to pursue. He was disinterested in the passing parade of fads and trends, concentrating on those principles affecting a person's relationship with God through Jesus Christ. Only by the disciplines of study and prayer could he say something of lasting relevance on that level. The timelessness of Tozer's writing is evidence of his success.

In reading one of Tozer's books, a person cannot help pause every so often, pick up his or her Bible and think more seriously about God. "Tozer," one reader observed, "is a conscience-keeper in regard to personal holiness, one's individual worship of God and one's daily, undiluted surrender of the soul to God."

Family pressure

One day Tozer's sons, Forrest and Wendell, took their father to lunch. The publishing firm of Harper & Row had been trying for seven years to get Tozer to do a book for them, but he had steadily refused because he was not in the business to make money. At lunch the two sons expressed to their father that they wanted their children to know that Tozer's books had been published by an established, intellectually recognized firm. They wanted their children to have something to be proud of. Tozer said nothing, but later went ahead and did a book for Harper & Row, *The Knowledge of the Holy.*

Tozer often wrote the first draft of a project by hand. He believed he could control the words better that way. Later, he would type out a second draft on his old portable Hermes typewriter. Usually his secretary typed the final draft. She sometimes served as a sounding board for his output.

One secretary in particular tried Tozer's patience, but he did not have the heart to replace her. He gave her a handwritten copy of an article he wanted typed. When she was finished, Tozer went to retrieve it.

"What did you think of that article?" Tozer asked inquisitively.

"Oh, Dr. Tozer," the woman apologized, "I didn't read it—I just typed it."

Tozer sadly shook his head and walked away.

TOZER-GRAMS

The minister in charge of the weekly meetings should take pains to see that the Word is read before the congregation in a voice clear enough to be understood and loud enough to be heard by all. To take great care for the sermon, and then for public reading grab the Bible and hastily turn to the first passage that looks inviting is to place the sermon above the Word of God itself.

The fashion now is to tolerate anything lest we gain the reputation of being intolerant. The tender-minded saints cannot bear to see Agag slain, so they choose rather to sacrifice the health of the Church for years to come by sparing error and evil; and this they do in the name of Christian love.

We would do well to seek a new appreciation of the inarticulate many who make up the body of the Church. They do a large share of the praying and pay most of the bills. Without them not a preacher could carry on, not a Bible school function. They are the flesh and sinews of the missionary program. They are the private soldiers of the Lord who do most of the fighting and get fewest decorations. The big stars of the Church get a lot of their glory now; the plain Christians must wait till the Lord returns. There will be some surprises then.

Religious habits can deceive the possessor as few things can do. As far as I know, a habit and a mud turtle are the only things in nature that can walk around after they are dead. For instance, many a man has returned thanks at the table faithfully for many years, and yet has never once really prayed from the heart during all that time. The life died out of the habit long ago, but the habit itself persisted in the form of a meaningless mumble.

PRAYER

Lord, make me childlike. Deliver me from the urge to compete with another for place or prestige or position. I would be simple and artless as a little child. Deliver me from pose and pretense. Forgive me for thinking of myself. Help me to forget myself and find my true peace in beholding Thee. That Thou mayest answer this prayer I humble myself before Thee. Lay upon me Thy easy yoke of self-forgetfulness that through it I may find rest. Amen.

"Meekness and Rest"
The Pursuit of God

PERSONAL GLIMPSES

Advice

Very few people went to Tozer for counseling—he was a preacher, not a pastor. I went once, though. As a seminary student I was looking for an assistant pastorate in the Chicago area. But when I approached the district superintendent, I was told, "We don't have anything to do with seminarians."

I went to Tozer and explained that I was a loyal member of the church and wanted to maintain ties with the Alliance. But the Alliance wasn't the kingdom of God, so if they wouldn't accept me I'd have to go elsewhere.

Tozer told me not to rush so fast, and two weeks later he offered me an assistant pastorate at the church.

Stan Lemon

I was preparing to go to Nyack College. Before I left there was one burning question I had in mind, and I went to Dr. Tozer and said, "Could you give me some advice concerning the problem of Calvinism versus Arminianism?"

And I'll never forget the advice he gave me. At the time I thought it was rather inconclusive and not too helpful. But I listened carefully. He said, "My son, when you get to college you're going to find that all of the boys will be gathered in a room discussing and arguing over Arminianism and Calvinism night after night after night. I'll tell you what to do, Cliff. Go to your room and meet God. At the end of four years you'll be way down the line and they'll still be where they started, because greater minds than yours have wrestled with this problem and have not come up with satisfactory conclusions. Instead, learn to know God."

Cliff Westergren

Cliff Westergren and I were commissioned for the mission field in the same service at Tozer's church. Tozer's humor and insight were displayed in a few brief words of advice just before the service.

Tozer came down the aisle to where Cliff and I were standing. To Cliff he said, "Just remember, life isn't all that serious." Turning to me, he tapped me on the side of the head and said, "Don't trust it."

Stan Lemon

"His writings are as fresh today as when he first wrote them. In his writings he left the superficial and the obvious and the trivial for others to toss around, giving himself to the discipline of study and prayer that resulted in articles and books that reached deep into the hearts of men."

Dr. Nathan Bailey
Late President
The Christian and Missionary Alliance

11

Editor

In 1946, A.W. Tozer was elected vice president of The Christian and Missionary Alliance, a position he held for four years. Dr. Harry M. Shuman was the president at the time and an old man. Tozer once confessed to a friend, "I sometimes see dear Brother Shuman walking across Times Square and realize that I am only one heartbeat away from becoming president." Tozer feared that Dr. Shuman would die and automatically he would become president. The thought was not a pleasant one for him so he resigned after his term, quite thankful that Dr. Shuman was still alive.

In 1950, two years after *The Pursuit of God* appeared, A.W. Tozer took on a new responsibility. He was named by The Christian and Missionary Alliance to be editor of its denominational publication, at that time called the *Alliance Weekly*.

The committee at the church's Council that brought in Tozer's name felt his "clear and forceful style and his unique presentation of a Christ-centered gospel would be approved by Bible-loving Christians everywhere." The opinion proved prophetic.

Ever since the magazine's first issue back in January, 1882, editorial responsibility had rested with men who had other full-time work. A.B. Simpson, who set the policy as the first editor, was pastor of the Gospel Tabernacle in New York City and also president of The Christian and Missionary Alliance. Tozer became editor without giving up his Chicago pastorate and with no appreciable cut-back in his slate of preaching engagements. The diminutive upstairs study behind Southside Alliance's pulpit became also an editorial office for the magazine.

When urged by some to resign from Southside Alliance and give full-time to the editorship, Tozer was adamant. "I can't give up the pastorate," he explained to a friend. "I need that discipline of preaching to the same congregation week after week. Without it, I would go stale. And if I don't preach, I have no material. When I prepare for the pulpit, then I can write editorials and articles."

That settled, Tozer went about reshaping what most

people regarded at the time as a rather stodgy house organ. In his first editorial, June 3, 1950, Tozer set the tone: "It will cost something to walk slow in the parade of the ages while excited men of time rush about confusing motion with progress. But it will pay in the long run, and the true Christian is not much interested in anything short of that."

As editor, it was Tozer's responsibility to write a weekly editorial for the magazine. This was an unsparing drain on his creative and spiritual energy. At times, with a deadline facing him, he would arrive in his study "as uninspired as a burnt shingle."

Clearing writer's block

Each writer has his or her own way to get the creative juices flowing. For Tozer, he would get his Bible and hymn book from his desk, walk over to the sofa in one corner of his office, kneel there and begin worshiping God. He would read from the Bible and read or softly sing a few hymns. He especially liked the hymns of Isaac Watts and Charles Wesley. By his own confession, he sang—on his knees—one of A.B. Simpson's songs almost every day.

Releasing his spirit to God, he would soon be enveloped in God's presence. Ideas would begin to come. He would pick up his pencil and, as it was in penning *The Pursuit of God*, he would write as fast as he could to keep up with what was being poured into his soul. Within an hour, sketches of two, three or even four editorials would be before him. Later he would meticulously polish these for publication.

Tozer was a stylist and a perfectionist. He determined that the magazine he edited would set an example that could profitably be followed by other religious publications. He insisted on clean, artistic layout, the use of only the best pictures, a professional literary style, a tone which he described as "dignified casualness." Lame attempts at humor, anything in bad taste, unverified reports, poor illustrations, bad poetry and clichés were avoided at any cost. At the same time, the magazine should be cordial, free and friendly and the style easy and sometimes even colloquial.

Tozer was severely self-critical, never truly satisfied with an issue, never pronouncing an issue good enough. To him anything short of perfection was unsatisfactory.

The story—allegedly true—still gets repeated occasionally about the woman who wrote to commend Tozer on the changes he had brought to the denominational organ. "But I hope," she concluded, "that you never change the size of the magazine. Not only do I like it, but my bird likes it, too. It fits nicely in the bottom of its cage."

Whatever the magazine's utility potential, it was welcomed by readers within The Christian and Missionary Alliance and far beyond for its incisive, prophetic editorial voice. It may be the only magazine ever to be bought primarily for its editorials. People who knew nothing of The Christian and Missionary Alliance subscribed just to read Tozer's editorials and stimulating articles. Tozer made the magazine.

And the magazine also made Tozer. It gave him a platform from which to speak to the issues of the day.

It helped to establish him as a spiritual leader far beyond the boundaries of a single church congregation or even a single denomination. He consistently called believers to return to the authentic, biblical positions that had characterized the Christian church when it was most faithful to Christ and His Word. He belonged to the whole church. He embraced true Christianity wherever he found it.

Tozer's editorials were published simultaneously in England. H.F. Stevenson, editor of the London-based *Life of Faith* magazine, said at Tozer's death, "His survey of the contemporary scene was as relevant to Britain as to his own country; his articles and books were read avidly here also."

The magazine almost ended Tozer's influence prematurely. Two years into his editorship, he suffered a heart attack. Although there was no organic damage, doctors ordered him to rest for several months, which he did.

Busy schedule costly

To say that his schedule was busy is to put it mildly. Tozer pastored the Alliance church in Chicago and later Toronto, edited the official magazine of the Alliance, preached at most of the major Bible conferences in the country, preached weekly over the WMBI radio station in Chicago and wrote books. He carried his load with a finesse and confidence that amazed many. Add to this schedule a somewhat fragile constitution and a person wonders how he was able to stand the pressure. But by 1952 the pressure was too great and he suffered the heart attack, which took him out of commission for several months. He convalesced in Florida with his friend Robert W. Battles.

Alliance Life, December 10, 1952, carried this explanation for its readers: "We wish to request the prayers of our readers in behalf of our Editor, Dr. A.W. Tozer. He has carried a very heavy schedule for the past two and a half years since he assumed the editorship of [*Alliance Life*] in addition to his pastoral responsibilities, and this has put considerable strain upon him physically. On Saturday, November 22, following a radio broadcast, Dr. Tozer became so ill that he was taken to the hospital. Examinations show that though there has been severe strain upon the heart there is no organic damage. He has, however, been ordered to take a complete rest. Please pray that God will strengthen and heal him quickly."

In 1954 Tozer's first term as elected *Alliance Life* editor was coming to a close. Perhaps health concerns prompted his action—he did not say—but he tendered his resignation, to the shock of officials at denominational headquarters. At least one of them, William F. Smalley, urged him in the strongest terms to reconsider. "It is my strong feeling," Smalley wrote in a letter to Tozer, "that your ministry in connection with the magazine has been of great blessing to the organization and a wonderful impetus."

Tozer's response evidenced no change of mind. "It grieves me very much to have to disappoint so many of my good friends. I am afraid they will feel that I am letting them down, but every man knows his own problems better than even his friends can know.

Thank you for your unfailing kindness to me and your deep unselfish interest in my ministry."

Despite his resignation, when the church Council convened that year, Tozer allowed himself to be reelected. He continued to be editor until his death nine years later in 1963.

Not without criticism

Subsequently, Tozer would face a very different reaction from a minority within the denomination. Tozer was never one to be too concerned about labels. He was more concerned about practical theology than how it is described. Referring to Max I. Reich, a converted Jewish rabbi who was a teacher at Moody Bible Institute, he remarked to a friend: "He loves the Lord and he has the fullness of the Holy Spirit. He wouldn't explain it our way, but he is filled with the Spirit." Tozer did not care too much about terminology so long as the spiritual experience was genuine.

Not all pastors within The Christian and Missionary Alliance were pleased with Tozer's openness to those who did not toe the denominational line. They did not like the direction in which he was taking their denominational magazine. They thought it should be more of a house organ, focusing on Alliance activities. They complained that Tozer was speaking to the whole world and not just to The Christian and Missionary Alliance. A few also objected to Tozer's generous use of the medieval mystics whose writings delighted him so.

The opposition came to a head in 1960 with a

feeble attempt to shut down the magazine for a year. It was a transparent move to get Tozer out of the editorship; a year later the magazine would be relaunched as a house organ. The move failed, and Tozer remained in command. But the attempt to unseat him was a wound that hurt deeply. "There goes one more idol," he later confided to a friend.

The early 1960s saw the magazine at its height of popularity. Circulation was up, and the quality of the publication continued to improve. Although Tozer was at the recognized age of retirement, there was no decline in the quality and vigor of his writing or his preaching.

That was as Tozer wanted it to be. "Pray," he asked his congregation, "that I won't become a feeble old preacher going around with a manila folder full of faded clippings, proud of what I used to be."

TOZER-GRAMS

Altar services are often rushed through in noisy haste, with a little sniffle on the part of the seeker being accepted as proof that a work of God has been done. We are so pitifully eager to get people "through" that we encourage them to "believe" and "praise" when as yet they are still in darkness.

We dare not be satisfied with any evangelism, however well organized and widely publicized, till it begins to produce results we can "handle" a week or a year later.

It will be a new day for us when we put away false notions and foolish fears and allow the Holy Spirit to fellowship with us as intimately as He wants to do, to talk to us as Christ talked to His disciples by the sea of Galilee. After that there can be no more loneliness, only the glory of the never-failing Presence.

PRAYER

O Lord, I have heard a good word inviting me to look away to Thee and be satisfied. My heart longs to respond, but sin has clouded my vision till I see Thee but dimly. Be pleased to cleanse me in Thine own precious blood, and make me inwardly pure, so that I may with unveiled eyes gaze upon Thee all the days of my earthly pilgrimage. Then shall I be prepared to behold Thee in full splendor in the day when Thou shalt appear to be glorified in Thy saints and admired in all them that believe. Amen.

"The Gaze of the Soul"
The Pursuit of God

"Praying with Tozer was a unique experience. I was delighted the first time he invited me to join him in his study for a time of prayer. After discussing some portion of Scripture over which he recently had been meditating, he suggested we pray. As a much younger man, I waited to see what posture he would take in order that I might comply.

"To my surprise he rose from his chair and stepped to the middle of his study and knelt down. I did the same. There, kneeling erect with no chair or table for support, we prayed facing one another for the next half hour. Thinking back now I recall clearly that the physical feat involved in the spiritual exercise left no room for mental woolgathering."

Robert Walker
Leaning into the Wind

12

A Man of Prayer

During a business session at a Christian and Missionary Alliance General Council, the delegates were bogged down in motions and amendments and amendments to amendments. Tozer became increasingly impatient with the tedium of it all. Finally, his restless spirit could take no more. He turned to Raymond McAfee sitting beside him.

"Come on, McAfee," he whispered, "let's go up to my room and pray before I lose all my religion."

Whatever acclaim he earned as an eloquent preacher and an outstanding writer can accurately be attributed to his close relationship with God. Tozer preferred God's presence to any other. The foundation of his Christian life was prayer. He not only preached prayer but practiced it. He always carried with him a small notebook in which he jotted requests for himself and others, usually of a spiritual nature.

Tozer's prayers bore the same marks as his preaching: honesty, frankness, humor, intensity. His praying deeply affected his preaching, for his preaching was but a declaration of what he discovered in prayer. His praying also affected his living. He often said, "As a man prays, so is he." Everything he did flowed from his prayer life.

The bulk of his time each day was spent wrestling with God in prayer. Tozer literally practiced the presence of God. Often he would withdraw from family and friends to spend time alone with God. It was not unusual for him to lose all track of time in those meetings with God.

McAfee regularly met in Tozer's study each Tuesday, Thursday and Saturday morning for a half hour of prayer. Often when McAfee would enter, Tozer would read aloud something he recently had been reading—it might be from the Bible, a hymnal, a devotional writer or a book of poetry. Then he would kneel by his chair and begin to pray. At times he prayed with his face lifted upward. Other times he would pray totally prostrated on the floor, a piece of paper under his face to keep him from breathing carpet dust.

God's presence

McAfee recalls one especially memorable day. "Tozer knelt by his chair, took off his glasses and laid them on the chair. Resting on his bent ankles, he clasped his hands together, raised his face with his eyes closed and began: 'O God, we are before Thee.' With that there came a rush of God's presence that filled the room. We both worshiped in silent ecstasy and wonder and adoration. I've never forgotten that moment, and I don't want to forget it."

On occasions while McAfee was praying, he would hear Tozer rustling about. Opening an eye to see what was going on, he would discover Tozer, pencil in hand, writing. While McAfee was praying, Tozer had a thought he wanted to capture.

Tozer met with his church staff regularly for prayer. Once, during a staff prayer meeting, Tozer was prone on the floor in deep conversation with God. The telephone rang. Tozer broke off his prayer to answer the phone. He carried on about a twenty-minute conversation with a pastor giving him all sort of instructions and advice that he himself never followed—taking time off, going on a vacation and so on. The staff just sat there listening and chuckling to themselves because Tozer never took a vacation in his life.

Hanging up the telephone Tozer resumed his position on the floor and picked up where he left off by saying, "Now, God, as I was saying . . . ."

Once Dr. Louis L. King, Tozer and two other preachers were engaged in a half day of prayer. One of the preachers was known for his bombastic, colorful speech both in his preaching and his praying. This man began praying for a certain world leader who at the time was hindering missionary work. "If you can't change him," the preacher prayed, "then kill him and take him to heaven!" Later Tozer took King aside. "Did you hear what he prayed this morning?" he asked, a hurt expression on his face. " 'Take him to heaven'? Why he doesn't even believe in Jesus Christ. That wasn't prayer. He was saying that for our benefit. You never speak to God in that fashion. When you approach God you should always use reverent language. It's God, not man, we're talking to in prayer!"

A sacred occupation

Prayer, according to Tozer, was the most sacred occupation a person could engage in. Often when Tozer prayed people felt as though God was right at his elbow. Sometimes they were tempted to open their eyes to see.

Tozer's praying embraced the minutiae as well as the transcendental. One time, while King was visiting, Tozer had to go downtown to buy some special light bulbs for the church. Before the two men left the office Tozer had them both kneel. In the most simple terms, he prayed, "Now, Lord, we don't know anything about light bulbs." And on he went in a very human way to ask God for wisdom in such a mundane matter as the purchase of light bulbs.

Summer Bible camps and conferences were a special delight to Tozer. Every year he spent considerable time ministering at these places. To him, the whole atmosphere was conducive to prayer and getting closer to God.

He usually would walk out each morning to the surrounding woods to find a place to pray. Kneeling beside a fallen log he would spend time in worship and prayer. On occasions another person would join him in these rustic prayer meetings. As they began Tozer would have some word to say about coming into the presence of God, which to him was always very real and immediate. Then he would invariably say, "Well, what shall we pray about?" Then followed a brief time of talking about subjects of prayer. Usually Tozer prayed first.

One morning the rain changed his usual plans so he and Robert W. Battles, a close friend, met in Tozer's cabin for prayer at 9 o'clock. Dr. Battles was sharing the conference platform with Tozer. Each knelt on opposite sides of a cot.

"Well, Junior," Tozer asked, "what should we pray for today?"

"I think we should pray for these people who have come to hear the likes of us preach."

The two men talked about prayer and what and

who they should be praying for. Then Tozer began to talk about God, the incarnation, the glory and majesty of the Trinity, holiness, heaven, angels, immortality, the church and its mission in the world. No agenda, no sense of time, only the marvelous sense of the presence of God.

Then, before they got around to actually praying, the lunch bell rang.

"Oh, no!" Battles complained. "We didn't even get down to praying and the bell has rung for lunch!"

"Well, Junior. We met to pray. Do you know something? What we have been doing all morning has been perilously close to praying."

There were times as the two men tramped through the nearby woods for a quiet walk together that Tozer would get a far-off look in his eye, his nostrils would flare and he would say in all solemnity, "Junior, I want to love God more than anyone in my generation."

At least once, Tozer lost all track of time as he was in his cabin praying. Time came for him to speak and he was nowhere to be found. Another person had to substitute for him. When Tozer finally did show up, he would only say that he had a more important appointment.

Focus on God

In prayer Tozer would shut out everything and everyone and focus on God. His mystic mentors taught him that. They showed him how to practice daily the presence of God. He learned the lesson well.

Prayer for Tozer was inextricably tied to worship. "Worship," said Tozer in an uncharacteristically long sentence, "is to feel in your heart and express in some appropriate manner a humbling but delightful sense of admiring awe and astonished wonder and overpowering love in the presence of that most ancient Mystery, that majesty which philosophers call the First Cause but which we call Our Father in Heaven."

Worship was the impetus behind all he was and did. It controlled every aspect of his life and ministry. "Labor that does not spring out of worship," he would admonish, "is futile and can only be wood, hay and stubble in the day that shall try every man's work."

Rebelling against the hectic schedules that kept his fellow ministers and fellow Christians from true worship, Tozer wrote, "I am convinced that the dearth of great saints in these times, even among those who truly believe in Christ, is due at least in part to our unwillingness to give sufficient time to the cultivation of the knowledge of God. . . . Our religious activities should be ordered in such a way as to leave plenty of time for the cultivation of the fruits of solitude and silence."

Tozer was an ardent lover of hymns and had in his library a collection of old hymnals. Often, on his way to an appointment he would meditate on one of the old hymns.

"Get a hymn book," he frequently advised as he counseled people. "But don't get one that is less than a hundred years old!" His Chicago church did not use the denomination's *Hymns of the Christian Life*. Instead, the congregation sang from a River Brethren

Church hymnal. Tozer preferred it because it contained more of the great hymns that he loved, and he enjoyed hearing his people sing them.

"After the Bible," he said in an *Alliance Life* article aimed at new Christians, "the next most valuable book is a good hymnal. Let any new Christian spend a year prayerfully meditating on the hymns of Watts and Wesley alone, and he or she will become a fine theologian." Then he added, "Afterward, let that person read a balanced diet of the Puritans and the Christian mystics. The results will be more wonderful than he could have dreamed." This was his personal pattern, year after year.

During the 1950s, Tozer found a kindred spirit in a plumber from Ireland, Tom Haire, a lay preacher. Haire became the subject of seven articles Tozer wrote for *Alliance Life* entitled "The Praying Plumber from Lisburn," later reissued as a booklet. Two men could hardly have been more different, yet their love for God and their sense of His worth drew them together.

Once, while Haire was visiting Chicago, Tozer's church was engaged in a night of fasting and prayer. Haire joined them. In the middle of the night, he got thirsty and went out for a cup of tea. Some church members felt Tom, by so doing, had "yielded to the flesh." Tozer disagreed. He saw in that act the beautiful liberty Tom enjoyed in the Lord.

Just before Haire was to return to his homeland, he stopped by Chicago to say good-bye.

"Well, Tom," Tozer remarked, "I guess you'll be going back to Ireland to preach."

"No," Tom replied in his thick Irish brogue. "I intend to cancel all appointments for the next six months and spend that time preparing for the judgment seat of Christ while I can still do something about it." It was an attitude not uncharacteristic of Tozer himself.

TOZER-GRAMS

If one-tenth of one per cent of the prayers made in any American city on any Sabbath day were answered, the world would see its greatest revival come with the speed of light. We seem to have gotten used to prayers that produce nothing. God still hears prayer and all the promises are still good, yet we go on at a pretty dying rate. Can someone tell us the answer?

I had been naive enough to believe that we had been disillusioned by the sorry performances of the personality boys of a few years ago, and that we had recovered from that form of abnormal psychology which we caught from the movies; but evidently I was too optimistic. Like malaria it's back on us again.

The first work of revealed truth is to secure an unconditional surrender of the sinner to the will of God. Until this has been accomplished, nothing really lasting has been done at all. The reader may admire the rich imagery of the Bible, its bold figures and impassioned flights of eloquence; he may enjoy

its tender musical passages, and revel in its strong homely wisdom; but until he has submitted to its full authority over his life, he has secured no good from it yet.

PRAYER

O God, I have tasted Thy goodness, and it has both satisfied me and made me thirsty for more. I am painfully conscious of my need of further grace. I am ashamed of my lack of desire. O God, the Triune God, I want to want Thee; I long to be filled with longing; I thirst to be made more thirsty still. Show me Thy glory, I pray thee, that so I may know Thee indeed. Begin in mercy a new work of love within me. Say to my soul, "Rise up, my love, my fair one, and come away." Then give me grace to rise and follow Thee up from this misty lowland where I have wandered so long. In Jesus' Name, Amen.

"Following Hard after God"
The Pursuit of God

PERSONAL GLIMPSES

Preaching

I remember certain things about Dr. Tozer's sermon delivery. He used to stand on his toes. He was a little man, so he used to stand on his toes frequently. It was his way of feeling part of what he was saying. And I especially remember the way he held his Bible. He would begin with the Bible laid flat on the pulpit. He would stick closely to his notes. Maybe 15 or 20 minutes into his message he would then pick up the Bible in one hand and hold it before him. He would stand away from the pulpit and preach for maybe the next 15 minutes. After that he would return the Bible to pulpit, stand back and never use a note for the remainder of the sermon. Now he was in high gear, the subject was his, and he was free to elucidate the truth.

Cliff Westergren

I was a young minister attending my very first Council in Long Beach, California. I was overwhelmed with the thought of listening to Dr. Tozer preach. As he came to the conclusion of his message the air was totally electrified. I was accustomed to altar calls and was fully expecting to see a mass movement forward. That surely would have been the case had he chosen to do so. Rather, in his inimitable but brusque manner he announced, "Don't come down here to the altar and cry about it—go home and live it." With that comment he dismissed the meeting. I was so impressed with that admonition, and profoundly moved, that I have remembered it for over 35 years. On numerous occasions it has challenged me to put "shoe leather" to my Christianity.

Earl M. Swanson

"Dr. D. Martyn Lloyd-Jones and I were discussing the mystics over dinner one evening and he related an interesting experience. With his permission I repeat it here.

" 'Dr. Tozer and I shared a conference years ago,' he said, 'and I appreciated his ministry and his fellowship very much. One day he said to me, "Lloyd-Jones, you and I hold just about the same position on spiritual matters, but we have come to this position by different routes." '

" 'How do you mean?' I asked.

" 'Well,' Tozer replied, 'you came by way of the Puritans and I came by way of the mystics.' And, you know, he was right!"

Warren W. Wiersbe
Walking With The Giants

13

Mystic and Prophet

Tozer's passion for God led him to the Christian mystics. In his day their writings were not popular, even among the clergy. But Tozer discovered that these great souls, however flawed their theology, were uncontrollably in love with God. His own pursuit of God put him in their debt.

The writings of these Christian mystics Tozer wove like threads of silver and gold into the fabric of his discourses. He cited them, paraphrased them, imitated them. He breathed their spirit, he relied upon their support. "These people," he would say, "know God, and I want to know what they know about God and how they came to know it." He so identified with the struggles and triumphs of certain devotional writers that many people referred to him, also, as a mystic—a label to which he never objected.

Utter devotion to God

Tozer's list of these "friends of God" grew with the years. Nothing delighted him more than to discover some long forgotten devotional writer, and he was always eager to introduce these discoveries to others. His admiration for their writings was not an endorsement of everything they did or taught, he was careful to point out. It was their utter devotion to God and their ability to share their spiritual insights that he valued.

Once in a sermon, Tozer referred to Lady Julian of Norwich as his girlfriend. The statement raised many eyebrows. "I think," Tozer explained, "that anyone who has been dead for more than 500 years is safe to be called a girlfriend." He discovered in her writings an attitude and passion for God that corresponded with his own spiritual quest.

"The word *mystic,*" Tozer explains in his introduction to *The Christian Book of Mystical Verse,* "refers to that personal spiritual experience common to the saints of Bible times and well known to multitudes of people in the postbiblical era. I refer to the evangelical mystic who has been brought by the gospel into intimate fellowship with the Godhead. His theology is no less and no more than is taught in the Christian Scriptures. He walks the high road of truth where walked of old prophets and apostles, and where down the centuries walked martyrs, reformers, Puritans, evangelists and missionaries of the cross.

"[The mystic] differs from the ordinary orthodox Christian only because he experiences his faith down in the depths of his sentient being while the other does not. He exists in a world of spiritual reality. He is quietly, deeply and sometimes almost ecstatically aware of the presence of God in his own nature and in the world around him. His religious experience is something elemental, as old as time and the creation. It is immediate acquaintance with God by union with the Eternal Son. It is knowing that which passes knowledge."

The word *mystic* did not scare Tozer. The term *mysticism* simply means "the practice of the presence of God," the belief that the heart can commune with God directly, moment by moment, without the aid of outward ritual. He saw this belief at the very core of real Christianity, the sweetest and most soul-satisfying experience a child of God can know.

Tozer was an enthusiastic admirer of Francois de Salignac de la Mothe Fenelon, the 17th-century

French saint whose eloquent sermons contributed greatly to the spiritual education of his contemporaries and whose generosity did much to mitigate the sufferings caused by the war of the Spanish-French Succession. Fenelon was a man who knew God, who lived in Him as a bird lives in the air. Providentially, he was endowed with the ability to lead others into the same kind of life. In Fenelon there was no trace of the morbidity that has marked some of the men and women who have been known as mystics.

Encouraged others to read mystics

When Harper & Row republished Fenelon's *Christian Counsel* under the title *Christian Perfection*, Tozer was delighted. He wrote an article on the subject, urging *Alliance Life* readers to secure a copy. "Come [to the book]," he said, "with a spirit of longing. Without strong desire nothing will do you much good. Be determined to know God. Read only after prayer and meditation on the Word itself. The heart must be readied for this book, otherwise it will be like any other and have little effect.

"Come in an attitude of devotion, in silence and humble expectation. If possible, get alone to read it. The presence of even the dearest friend often distracts the heart and prevents complete concentration. Get surrendering and consecrating done before coming to Fenelon; he begins where others leave off. Be in earnest. Fenelon assumes the seriousness of his readers. If anyone should be infected with the strange notion that religion should afford amusement as well as salvation, let him or her pass Fenelon by. This book is for the person who thirsts after God. . . . Never read more than one chapter a day. It would be a mistake to hurry through the book. It is to be studied, meditated on, marked, prayed over and returned to as often and as long as it continues to minister to the soul."

For inner nourishment, Tozer turned constantly to these masters of the inner life. He sat long and lovingly at the feet of these saintly teachers drawing water from their wells with reverence and gratitude. He lifted thankful eyes to God for the men and women who taught him to desire the better way: Nicholas Herman of Lorriane, Nicholas of Cusa, Meister Eckhart, Frederick William Faber, Madame Jeanne Guyon. Only two stipulations did Tozer make: that his teachers must know God, as Carlyle said, "otherwise than by hearsay," and that Christ must be all in all to them.

Tozer discovered that the companionship of Christ had to be cultivated. That is why he withdrew so often and spent so much time alone. "You can be straight as a gun barrel theologically," Tozer often remarked, "and as empty as one spiritually." Perhaps that was why his emphasis was not on systematic theology but on a personal relationship with God. For him it was a relationship so real, so overpowering as to utterly captivate his attention. He longed for what he fondly referred to as a God-conscious soul—a heart aflame for God.

But the pursuit of God had its counterpart in proclamation. "Years ago," Tozer once said, "I prayed that God would sharpen my mind and enable me to receive everything He wanted to say to me. I then prayed that God would anoint my head with the oil of the prophet so I could say it back to people."

A call to modern-day prophets

In frequent lectures to young preachers he sought for those who would join his "Fellowship of the Burning Heart," who would pay the price and, like himself, take a mystical approach to the ministry. He issued a distinct call for modern-day prophets.

Tozer recognized there are in the church today many good men of spotless life—splendid, Spirit-filled teachers. "I'm profoundly grateful for these men and have benefited from their ministry," he would say. "But I believe the times call for a few men who will be specially anointed and endued with gifts peculiarly suited to the needs of this hour. These men will know the mind of God for their day and will speak with calm assurance. They will be in one sense prophets to their generation."

"It will cost you everything to follow the Lord," Tozer told these young men, "and it will cost you more to be God's man for the hour. Anybody can go around and teach the Bible. Many do it and do it well. Many pastors do well in building up a congregation by Bible teaching, and we need Bible teaching and Bible teachers. But there is a tremendous need for prophets in each generation. These are the spiritual originals, the God-intoxicated few, who, in every age, have spoken God's clear message into the duller ears of the multitudes."

Tozer emphasized the importance of teaching people how to worship God. "Lead them," he advised, "away from the frivolous to a meaningful, dignified worship service. Teach them to sing some of the old hymns of the church—hymns that glorify God, hymns with some meaning to them."

Once at a Bible conference he testified to a spiritual experience he had as a young preacher. "A preacher friend joined me for a walk out in the woods for private Bible reading and prayer. He stopped at a log and, if I know him, probably fell asleep. I went on a little farther, as Jesus did, and knelt down and began to read my Bible. I was reading about the camp of Israel in the wilderness and how God laid it out in a beautiful diamond pattern. All at once I saw God as I never saw Him before. In that wooded sanctuary I fell on my face and worshiped. Since that experience, I have lost all interest in cheap religious thrills. The vacuous religious choruses we sing hold no attraction for me. I came face-to-face with the sovereign God, and since that time only God has mattered in my life."

In his early ministry Tozer recognized that the anointing oil of the prophet was upon him. It humbled him, but more than that it drove him to his knees. Often during the early years in Chicago he would take a morning streetcar out to Lake Michigan, only his Bible with him, and spend the day in solitude with God.

Tozer could speak prophetically because he had encountered God. He earned his reputation as a 20th century prophet and functioned, as someone observed, as the "conscience of evangelicalism" not only in his own generation but for the generations that have succeeded him.

TOZER-GRAMS

Some people spend all their time on a kind of doctrinal trapeze and never come down long enough to learn how to walk with God. Out our way they swing by their toes on the flying bar of divine sovereignty, turn a double summersault, catch hold of the eternal decrees, and come up bowing on the mystery of predestination. It may be good exercise (though I suspect a little strenuous for the average heart), but I have not noticed that it makes them any holier or more Christlike. The wise words of Thomas a Kempis should not be forgotten: "It is better to feel compunction than to know the definition thereof."

Just before he died I heard Dr. Reuben A. Torrey preach a sermon on the Holy Spirit. He was pretty feeble and his voice was shaky, but it was one of the greatest sermons I have ever heard, and after the passing of years the fragrance lingers. One sentence particularly remains: "We do not need to worry about getting more of the Holy Spirit, but see to it that He gets more of us. We can have all of Him if He can get all of us." That is worth pondering.

On the pulpit of a famous mission appears the text: "Sirs, we would see Jesus," a gentle reminder to the speaker to keep to his subject, Christ and Him crucified. When the pulpit is used for any other purpose than to set forth the Word of God, the glory has departed. Let us keep the Bible in the pulpit, and as far as possible keep the donkeys out!

PRAYER

O God and Father, I repent of my sinful preoccupation with visible things. The world has been too much with me. Thou hast been here and I knew it not. I have been blind to Thy Presence. Open my eyes that I may behold Thee in and around me. For Christ's sake, Amen.

"The Universal Presence"
The Pursuit of God

"I fear that we shall never see another Tozer. Men like him are not college bred but Spirit taught. . . .

"Dr. Tozer is to me a classic example of the promise, 'Out of his inmost being shall flow rivers of living water.' "

Leonard Ravenhill

14

Poetry and the Poets

Poet Percy Bysshe Shelley described poetry as the record of the best and happiest moments of the happiest and best minds. Anatole France compared a beautiful poem to a violin bow drawn across the fibers of our souls, setting not only the thoughts of the poet but our own souls to singing. Those who produced it often did so at great personal sacrifice. Wordsworth confessed that his poetry never brought in enough to buy shoestrings.

King David is renowned for many conquests on the field of battle. His youthful struggle with Goliath has excited succeeding generations of children and the story of his friendship with Jonathan is classic. But today that which towers above all accomplishments of this great man is a little poem he wrote, "The 23rd Psalm." The notes of this sweet song will never cease to echo down the corridors of time. Yet it is but one of the many inspiring bequests from a man who held the golden pen of a ready writer, selected a good matter to indict and tested his lyrics on the vibrant strings of his harp.

Tozer was an ardent admirer of poets and a true lover of their works. He was drawn to them because like himself they placed the good things of life on a pedestal above money and ease; they bore a soul burden that had to be unloaded. While not venturing far into the field himself, Tozer did write some poetry. Two compositions were set to music and sung on a number of occasions by Raymond McAfee.

Word of the Father
(Music: Schubert's "Ave Maria")

Word of the Father! Light of light;
Eternal praise is Thine alone;
Strong in Thy uncreated might,
Sweet with a holy fragrance all Thine own.
The dark beginnings of creation
Had their first rise and spring in Thee;
The universe, Thy habitation,
Which art, and evermore shalt be.
Word of the Father!

Word of the Father! Truly God,
And truly man by incarnation,

Born to endure the thorns, the rod,
The shameful wounds for our salvation.
Our sins, our woes come all before us,
We have no friend, no friend but Thee;
O spread Thy saving mantle o'er us,
And set our mourning spirits free.
  Word of the Father!

Word of the Father! Hear our prayer!
Send far the evil tempter from us,
And make these souls Thy tender care
Lest sin and Satan overcome us.
O conquering Christ! Deep hell, despairing,
Must bow and own Thy right to reign,
When Thou, with joy beyond comparing
Shalt bring Thy ransomed ones again.
  Word of the Father!

Out of the Depths
(Music: Massenet's "Elegy")

Out of the depths do I cry,
  O God, to Thee!
Hide now Thy face from my sin!
Fountains of tears flow in vain;
  So dark the stain
Tears cannot wash it away.
Bearing the shame in my heart;
Broken with anguish I mourn all the day,
Grief my companion the lonely night through.

Though I have gone far astray,

Turn not away;
Lord, I have hoped in Thy Word.
Think on Thy mercy and rescue my soul
Now lest I die!

High as the heavens above,
Deep as the sea,
Lord, is Thy goodness to me.
Faithful art Thou to forgive,
Now shall I live
To sing of Thy wonderful love.
Thou hast redeemed me,
Through grace I am Thine,
O joy divine,
Thine evermore.

One of Tozer's last literary efforts was collecting an anthology of poems. Published by Christian Publications shortly after his death, the collection became *The Christian Book of Mystical Verse.* Tozer's love of poetry—both sacred and secular—is evident in all his works. In several of his books each chapter opened with a prayer and closed with a poem.

Among secular poets, Tozer was particularly fond of such nature poets as Wordsworth, who saw God in creation. But instead of proceeding through nature to God, as many poets did, Tozer went from God to nature. While he confessed his indebtedness to the nature poets, he felt that no true Christian could read them without feeling disappointed. They spoke of God, but only second hand. Theirs was not the God of the Bible as revealed in Jesus Christ, but a vague, shadowy being almost indistinguishable from the forces of nature.

> Wisdom and Spirit of the universe!
> Thou soul that art the eternity of thought
> That givest to forms and images a breath
> And everlasting motion.
> "Prelude," William Wordsworth

For better perspective Tozer turned from the purest nature poets to the prophets and psalmists of Scripture. These saw God first; they rose by the power of faith to the throne of the Majesty on high and observed the created world from above. Their love of natural objects was deep and intense, but they loved them not for their own sakes but for the sake of Him who created them. They walked through the world as through the garden of God. Everything reminded them of Him. They saw His power in the tempest; they heard His voice in the thunder; the mountains told them of His strength, and the rocks reminded them that He was their hiding place.

Although he clearly saw God in nature, Tozer was more intent on the new heaven and new earth than on this present world. In an editorial entitled "The World to Come," Tozer noted that we are all headed toward another world. How unutterably wonderful that we Christians have one of our own kind to go ahead and prepare a place for us! That place will be divinely ordered, beyond death, where nothing can hurt or make afraid, he reminded. He closed his editorial with lines by Bernard of Cluny:

Jerusalem the glorious!
The glory of the elect!
O dear and future vision
That eager hearts expect!
Even now by faith I see thee,
Even here thy walls discern;
To thee my thoughts are kindled,
And strive, and pant, and yearn.

Tozer did "strive, and pant, and yearn" after that future Jerusalem and the reign of God. "My soul followeth hard after thee" (Psalm 63:8 KJV) succinctly states Tozer's foremost interest always: he pursued God. Not that he did not already know Him—to have found God and still pursue Him is the soul's paradox of love. St. Bernard of Clairvaux wrote about this holy paradox in a musical quatrain that Tozer dearly loved:

We taste Thee, O Thou Living Bread,
And long to feast upon Thee still:
We drink of Thee, the Fountainhead
And thirst our souls from Thee to fill.

Frederick W. Faber was a favorite poet also, and Tozer included 20 of his poems in *The Christian Book of Mystical Verse.* The measure in which God revealed Himself to Faber's seeking heart set his whole life afire with burning adoration. It was this complete enthrallment with God that so enamored Tozer.

Among Faber's works Tozer found a hymn to the

Holy Spirit that he ranked among the finest ever written. He wondered why it had never been set to music and sung in churches. "Can the reason be," he asked, "that it embodies personal experience of the Holy Spirit so deep and intimate, so fiery hot that it corresponds to nothing in the hearts of present-day worshipers?"

> Fountain of Love! Thyself true God!
> Who through eternal days
> From Father and from Son hast flowed
> In uncreated ways!
>
> O Light! O Love! O very God
> I dare no longer gaze
> Upon thy wondrous attributes
> And their mysterious ways.

Another of Tozer's favorites by Faber was this hymn in celebration of God's eternity:

> Thou hadst no youth, great God,
> An Unbeginning End Thou art;
> Thy glory in itself abode,
> And still abides in its own tranquil heart:
> No age can heap its outward years on Thee:
> Dear God! Thou art Thyself Thine own eternity.

Tozer warned, "Do not skip this merely as another poem. The difference between a great Christian and any other kind lies in the quality of our religious concepts, and the ideas expressed in these six lines can be like rungs on Jacob's ladder leading upward to a sounder and more satisfying idea of God." Faber became Tozer's mentor in the sound ideas of God.

But Tozer's love of poetry did not stop with those describing God; it went on to poems that enunciated the human experience as well. Tozer knew that the way of the cross is unpopular and brings a measure of reproach on those who take it. Rarely do separated Christians escape a certain amount of hatred in their lifetimes. After they have been dead a while, time and distance may soften the lines of the portrait and the world that hated them while they lived will sometimes praise them when they are gone. John Wesley and his Methodists are good examples of this strange phenomenon. They were scorned and derided while on earth, considered offscourings to be persecuted or worse. But now we sing their hymns and build their sepulchers. History records the abuses heaped upon them for their "perfectionism" and for their irrepressible joy that embarrassed people and made them hurry away.

Gerhard Tersteegen, whom Tozer never tired of quoting, in a hymn called "Pilgrim Song," sought to comfort and cheer the holy wayfarers passing unloved and unnoticed through the wilderness. The last stanza reads:

> We follow in His footsteps;
>   What if our feet be torn?
> Where He has marked the pathway
>   All hail the briar and thorn!
> Scarce seen, scarce heard, unreckoned,

Despised, defamed, unknown
Or heard but by our singing,
On, children! ever on!

Explained Tozer, "The world is big, tangled and dark, and we are never sure where a true Christian may be found. One thing we know: the more like Christ he is the less likely it will be that a newspaper reporter will be seeking him out. However much he may value the esteem of his fellow men, he may for the time be forced to stand under the shadow of their displeasure. Or the busy world may not even know he is there—except that they hear him singing."

Tozer drew heavily on poetry to illustrate theological concepts. For example, in an editorial entitled "Refined or Removed?" he said: "We Christians must look sharp that our Christianity does not simply refine our sins without removing them. The work of Christ as Savior is twofold: to save His people from their sins and to reunite them forever with the God from whom sin had alienated them. . . . Christian theologians have all recognized the necessity for an adequate purgation of a renewed nature to the believer before he is ready for the fellowship of God. Our hymnists also have seen and wrestled with this problem—and thanks be to God, have found the answer, too."

Thomas Binney had felt the weight of this problem and stated it along with the solution in a little-known but deeply spiritual hymn that Tozer recounted:

Eternal Light! Eternal Light!
How pure the soul must be

When, placed within Thy searching sight,
It shrinks not, but with calm delight
  Can live, and look on Thee.

O how shall I, whose native sphere
  Is dark, whose mind is dim,
Before the Ineffable appear,
And on my naked spirit bear
  The uncreated beam?

There is a way for man to rise
  To that sublime abode:
An offering and a sacrifice,
A Holy Spirit's energies,
  An Advocate with God.

Although Tozer clearly had his favorite writers—such as Faber—he read and appreciated many, including and perhaps especially those who were less well known. In *The Knowledge of the Holy*, Tozer quoted a Greek hymn to drive his point home. In other pieces he quoted Oliver Wendell Holmes, Christina Rossetti, Nicolaus Ludwig von Zinzendorf, Charles Wesley, Jeanne Marie Guyon, Thomas Moore, Isaac Watts and Alfred, Lord Tennyson. The list was varied and sometimes at odds with the list of "greats" esteemed by scholars. But each had an appreciation for God that Tozer valued.

One poet particularly admired by Tozer—though perhaps not as much for poetry as for his other accomplishments—was A.B. Simpson, founder of The Christian and Missionary Alliance. Approaching middle age, broken in health, Simpson became despondent and was ready to withdraw from the ministry. He chanced to hear the words of a simple Negro spiritual, which he later enlarged into a poem and a hymn:

> My Jesus is the Lord of Lords:
> No man can work like Him.

Simpson sought a place to rest, and after a protracted session with seeking God he went forth completely cured. Following this encounter he labored tirelessly for 35 years in the service of his Master. It was faith in the God of limitless power that provided the strength to carry on. Tozer emphasized this thought with a citation from still another poet, Sir John Bowring:

> Almighty One! I bend in dust before Thee;
> Even so veiled cherubs bend;
> In calm and still devotion I adore Thee,
> All-wise, all-present Friend.

Tozer's mix of poetry and straightforward editorial prose gave him a vehicle to explore the condition of humanity and reach the highest planes of worship. Indeed, worship, devotion and an acute awareness of the presence of God were his goals—and poetry was an effective means to that end.

TOZER-GRAMS

The greatest danger we face from this machine age is that we will become engrossed with mechanical gadgets and forget we have hearts. Man cannot live by bread alone nor by machinery alone. The heart must be nurtured. For this reason the prophet and the poet are more important to a nation than the engineer or the inventor. Longfellow and Whittier have meant more to us than Edison or Ford. Burns' songs have meant more to Scotland than Watts' steam engine.

Someone has advanced the idea that if we would have a revival, we should begin to sing; that revivals always come on the wings of song. It is true that revivals and song always go together, but the song is the effect of the revival, never the cause of it. Men are not revived because they sing; they sing because they are revived. It is coldness of heart that has caused us to lose the joy and zest from our singing. The revived heart will soon burst into song.

It would be well for us if we could learn early the futility of trying to obtain forbidden things by overpersuading God. He will not be thus stampeded. Anything that falls within the circle of His will He gives freely to whosoever asks aright, but not days or weeks of fasting and prayer will persuade Him to alter anything that has gone out of His mouth.

PRAYER

God of our fathers, enthroned in light, how rich, how musical is the tongue of England! Yet when we attempt to speak forth Thy wonders, our words how poor they seem and our speech how unmelodious. When we consider the fearful mystery of Thy Triune Godhead we lay our hand upon our mouth. Before that burning bush we ask not to understand, but only that we may fitly adore Thee, One God in Persons Three. Amen.

"The Holy Trinity"
The Knowledge of the Holy

"... late 20th century evangelicals see him as one of their uncompromising champions of the faith, a determined opponent of show and the checkmate of worldliness."

Dr. Louis L. King
A.W. Tozer: An Anthology

15

Family Man

In writing the biography of A.B. Simpson, Tozer emphasized the importance of retaining the "warts." Often when he spoke to groups of writers, he would labor the same point. "Writing is false," he stressed, "when virtues are overdrawn and blemishes are concealed."

As a family man, Tozer had his share of contradictions and incongruities.

Tozer was the product of his rural upbringing and its division of labor. His mother had major responsibility for the household and the children, himself included. His father devoted his attention to the farm work. Although urban church ministry was very different from the farm, Tozer saw his wife's role as essentially similar to his mother's.

Tozer's goal was God. His pursuit of God demanded that all else be secondary. After all, Jesus said, "Any of you who does not give up everything he has cannot be my disciple" (Luke 14:33). He also said, "Any one who loves his son or daughter more than me is not worthy of me" (Matthew 10:37). In a sense Tozer saw his family as a distraction from his supreme goal of knowing God.

Habitually Tozer became entirely engrossed in his work and derived wholesome pleasure from it. Sometimes he would become melancholy or moody when, for whatever reason, he was forced to quit it for a time. He never took vacations and rarely took even a day off.

One time Tozer did take an extended time off, however—he had all his teeth extracted. He was out of his pulpit for about five weeks and, true to his disposition, thought he might never preach again. At his first speaking engagement after the ordeal, Raymond McAfee introduced him at a church banquet. McAfee announced, "We will now hear some true words through false teeth."

"For the past five weeks I have been on vacation," Tozer responded dryly. "Some people go to the mountains. Some people go to the shore." He paused and looked around the audience. "I went to the dentist."

The scope of Tozer's ministry militated against a wholesome family life. Speaking engagements meant he was away more than he was home. When he was actually in the house, he was in his bedroom study reading or writing. Ada Tozer had the responsibility of raising the six boys, and that was how her husband felt it should be.

As a Bible conference speaker Tozer was in demand, so he was not much help with raising the boys. There were rare occasions when Tozer would assist his wife in the ironing. Mrs. Tozer would get him to help by agreeing to read to him while he would work. The picture conjured up is humorous: imagine Dr. Tozer wearing a frilly apron, ironing shirts while Mrs. Tozer is not far away in a rocking chair reading aloud *Christian Perfection* by Francois de Salignac de la Mothe Fenelon.

A car was unnecessary

Tozer's pursuit of God certainly eclipsed his interest in material things. He even gave up his car in 1934, public transportation being dependable. He explained to his boys, some of whom were just getting to driving age, that he couldn't afford the licenses, the frequent repairs, the gasoline or—most important—to ride around in style and comfort when many people in the church could hardly afford the seven cents fare on the streetcar. "Besides," Tozer explained, "I have found the half-hour streetcar ride between home and church to be a fine, uninterrupted reading time!" (Tozer once confided in a friend, "I don't want my boys when they come of age scrapping over who will drive it.")

Years later, on his birthday, the congregation gave Tozer a brand new automobile. Right on the spot he said, "I really don't need a car." With that he turned to the church's missionary treasurer and gave the car to missions.

But there was one place where Tozer's heavenly aspirations and materialism coincided. That was at the bookstore, especially the used bookstore. Tozer found it hard to pass up a used bookstore. On the rare times when he took a day off, he usually ended up at one of Chicago's used bookshops browsing for old volumes written by some saint not yet rediscovered.

While still pastoring in Indianapolis, Tozer invited a good friend, Dr. J.T. Zamrazil, to preach in a series of evangelistic meetings at his church. One afternoon, Tozer took Zamrazil downtown to show him a beautiful, leatherbound set of Emerson on display in the window of a bookstore. As the two young men stood at the window, Tozer talked at length about Emerson and what a good writer and thinker he was. Tozer had Emerson's complete works in his library, but his set was "ragged and almost worn out." Zamrazil could sense the temptation mounting in Tozer's mind.

Finally the two left to go somewhere else, but it was not long before Tozer decided he should return to the bookstore for another look at Emerson. They looked and again left, but Tozer could talk of nothing else. At last he said, "Let's go back for just one more look." That one more look was Tozer's undoing.

The two men lugged the set home. As they entered the parsonage, Tozer began excitedly to tell Ada about his latest acquisition.

"Oh, Daddy," Mrs. Tozer cut in, "how could you when you know the children need shoes and . . . "

By that time, Zamrazil had retreated to the guest room. Later, with a mischievous twinkle in his eye, Tozer presented his friend with his cast-off set of Emerson.

Target shooting

Physical activity was not a high priority for Tozer. As a young man he played a bit of golf, but not enthusiastically and not for long. The only sport that really interested him was target shooting. Up in his attic he erected a straw target, and occasionally he would mount the stairs to shoot a BB pellet pistol. On rare occasions he would venture out to a shooting range.

His concept of recreation was to go off by himself and read a good book. Sometimes he would buy a round-trip ticket on the train to give himself three or four hours of privacy for study and prayer. "The cost is worth it," he would reply if someone asked why he did it. "And besides, I like riding the train!"

When the Tozer family first arrived in Chicago, they moved into a modest Southside bungalow at 10735 Prospect Avenue, eventually converting the sun porch into a boys' dormitory. When the six boys left home, the Tozers found and moved to a larger house on Longwood Drive—about five miles from the church.

Since the family did not have a car, Ada Tozer, like many other women in Chicago, would take the bus or streetcar to do her grocery shopping. Always in tow by her side would be at least one small boy.

Once, returning from such a trip with her arms ladened with groceries, Ada stopped at a corner to give the right-of-way to a slow-moving streetcar. The son who happened to be with her that day, intrigued by the street car, released his hold on his mother's dress and ran and grabbed the moving car. It dragged him a short distance before the conductor, discovering the extra cargo, stopped the car and rescued his nonpaying passenger, little the worse for his bumpy ride.

"Here's your son, ma'am," he said to Mrs. Tozer as he delivered the bruised hitchhiker to his relieved and embarrassed mother. "I recommend you take him home and give him a good spanking."

Tozer himself rarely used physical discipline with his boys. "Now, boys," he would quietly instruct his sons, "we have rules here in our house, just like the Chicago Cubs have rules. And just like those baseball players, I expect you to follow and obey the rules."

Private talks

When there was a disciplinary problem that demanded his attention, he usually took the offender to his bedroom study for a private talk. Quietly, he would assure the erring son that he believed in him. Putting a hand on the boy's head, he would say, "I know I can trust you because you always tell me the truth." Overpowered by such a display of paternal confidence, the wayward boy would volunteer the facts, whereupon Tozer would affirm that the boy was better than to do such mischief. Wendell Tozer remembers that those private talks always "made you cry." He said, "We all would rather be treated to the lilac switch by our mother than to have a talking-to by our dad."

When the boys were small, Tozer would line up all six in a production line and wash their faces with Castile soap. "He was gentle and tender," Wendell recalls. "He had an even disposition—no highs or lows. There were never any outbursts in the home."

Tozer did not follow his sons' elementary and secondary education too closely, but he expected them to work hard and to develop their talents. College was something else. Wendell was still living at home while attending the University of Illinois. Tozer would get up early in the morning and prepare breakfast for just the two of them. During breakfast Tozer wanted to know what Wendell was learning at the university. "I was always surprised," Wendell said, "how well versed my father was in the subjects I was taking."

Tozer loved to discuss books and authors with Wendell. "He would ask my opinion of a book he liked, and if I didn't agree with him that it was a good book, he would say, 'When a book and a head come in contact and there is a hollow sound, you can't conclude that the book is empty.' "

At home there was no preaching and, in fact, little religious discussion. There was no discussion of doctrine at all, and no effort at formal or regular Scripture reading in a group setting such as might be called a family altar. But all the children were in church for the two services sitting with the adults every Sunday. The children also joined the lengthy, wide-roaming discussions that followed every Sunday dinner until Tozer signaled the end by announcing it was time to do the dishes. Words, their origins, shifting meanings and connotations, and their colors and tones and feel. Ideas and where they come from and how to separate them into their essential parts, and what else can be done with them to test them. These were the things most chewed on at every meal.

One of Tozer's sons, Stanley, followed him into the ministry, although it was not with The Christian and Missionary Alliance. At his son's ordination service Dr. Tozer was asked to preach. No doubt he did so with many mixed feelings, but Tozer was not one to give vent to emotions. He preached on "Moses at the Burning Bush," a sermon he had preached many times before at Bible conferences all over the country. It was a favorite of his.

Before the service, Dr. Tozer asked his son, "Do I have to wear one of those bathrobes?" referring, of course, to the robes worn by the clergy of that denomination.

"No, Dad," Stanley said. "You don't have to wear one if you don't want to. I really don't mind what you wear."

"Well," replied Tozer, "I guess I'll wear one, then." Knowing Tozer, if it would have been a requirement he would not have worn one. He was a rebel at heart in everything.

When Stanley graduated from seminary he came out with an earned doctoral degree. "I think my father," Stanley reflected, "was a little envious of my earned degree even though at the time he had two honorary degrees."

Checkers was a favorite pastime in the Tozer household. The boys were delighted when they could talk their father into playing a game or two with them. It was always a challenge of wits, and as the boys got older, they became harder to beat. Once Tozer became so engrossed in a checkers game with his sons that he forgot he had an engagement to speak at a Youth For Christ rally on the north side of Chicago. The meeting chairman, presuming Tozer had been delayed by heavy traffic, started the rally without him. Finally, in a state of near panic, he called the house. To his dismay, he discovered that Tozer was in the midst of a checkers game with one of his sons. By then there was no way he could make the engagement.

A daughter is born

In 1939, Ada Tozer gave birth to a girl, Rebecca. After six rambunctious boys and a nine-year hiatus, in their middle years the Tozers joyfully welcomed Becky into their home and hearts. Years later, in a sermon, Tozer reflected on that momentous event: "She was a lovely little thing. After raising six boys—it was just like trying to bring up a herd of buffaloes—this refined, feminine little lady came along with all her pretty, frilly things. She and I became sweethearts from the first day I saw her little red face through the glass in the hospital. I was 42 years old when she was born."

Tozer went on to tell how they dedicated Becky to the Lord. "We dedicated her formally in the church service, but she was still mine. Then the day came when I had to die to my Becky, my little Rebecca. I had to give her up and turn her over to God to take if He wanted her at any time. . . . When I made that awful, terrible dedication I didn't know but God would take her from me. But He didn't. . . . She was safer after I gave her up than she had ever been before. If I had clung to her I would have jeopardized her; but when I opened my hands and said with tears, 'You can have her, God, the dearest thing I have,' she became perfectly safe."

His or God's, Becky wrought remarkable changes in A.W. Tozer. The man who relegated to Ada Tozer most of the upbringing of his six sons suddenly became an extremely attentive father. Maybe too attentive—he found it difficult to discipline Becky. She was able to manipulate her father and, like any other little girl, did so every chance she got. All she had to do was blink her eyes, stick out a trembling lower lip and say softly, "Please, Daddy," and Tozer melted and gave in.

Tozer wove Becky into many of his sermon illustrations. She was the single most important person in his life. Often when he was away on a preaching mission, he would write letters not to his wife but to Becky.

Each Wednesday at Southside Alliance, the women of the church met all day to pray for foreign missionaries and to work on missionary projects. When Rebecca came along, Tozer volunteered to take care of her on Wednesdays so Ada could continue to participate in the Wednesday missionary activities.

On these Wednesdays when Becky was old enough

to go to school, Tozer would fix lunch for the two of them. Always it consisted of a fried hamburger patty apiece and fried potatoes. When Becky became a woman with a family of her own, she tried unsuccessfully to duplicate those fried potatoes. "They were the most delicious I have ever tasted," she remarked nostalgically.

Forrest Tozer, remembering a similar practice said, "I can still sense the fragrance of the onions cooking with them, coming out to greet me and quicken my step as I slogged home for lunch after a hard morning in the third grade."

During school vacations, Tozer would take Becky after Wednesday lunch for a walk in one of the several nearby parks. In a qualified sense, Tozer was a naturalist. During those walks, Tozer would identify trees and plants, insects and especially birds. He loved to watch birds. The walk usually ended at a drug store, where Becky would order a chocolate malt while Tozer settled for a plain vanilla shake.

A great storyteller

As he had with her brothers, Tozer also found time to tell Becky bedtime stores. "The thing I remember most about my father," she reflects, "was those marvelous stories he would tell me. He was a great storyteller. There was one series about a rabbit detective who would go all over the world on exciting adventures. The queen's jewels had been stolen, and the rabbit detective was commissioned to find them. Night after night, for several years, my father told this story, making it up each night. I wish I could have recorded it for my children. Those are fond memories of my father."

Later, when Becky became a teen, Tozer boasted to his friend, Robert W. Battles, of his high aspirations for his daughter. "I'm going to teach her all about nature and poetry and literature," he said. "She won't have any time for boys."

Not long after that, Tozer took Becky with him to a summer Bible camp where he was to speak. One evening after his message, he looked for his daughter. He could not find her anywhere. He enlisted Battles, also at the camp, to help him look for her.

"Junior, where do you suppose she is?" Tozer inquired seriously.

"Well, Father," joked Battles, "maybe she's off studying nature." Much to Tozer's chagrin, Becky was indeed studying nature—human nature. Becky had discovered boys, and there was nothing he could do about it. It was a sad day.

Time for family

One of the problems with Tozer's busy schedule was finding time for family. Often his ministry took him away from his family for lengthy periods. Even when Tozer was at home he spent much of his time in his second floor study either reading or writing. This created some tension in the family. Ada Tozer did much of the raising of the children. Because of her selfless sacrifice in this area, Dr. Tozer was able to develop the ministry that he had.

Mrs. Tozer was gracious, always with a sweet smile. She was a pretty woman, intelligent and well read. She was an excellent mother and freed Dr. Tozer from many family responsibilities to pursue his ministry. He could not have influenced the Christian world as he did without her.

Mrs. Tozer had a special interest in small children and the elderly. And she would go out of her way to pay attention to the often neglected and unsung people in the congregation. She always attended the Women's Missionary Prayer Fellowship of the church and sang in the choir.

Her family kept her quite busy. She had 46 shirts to do every week in an era before the advent of "wash and wear" fabrics. Even with a mangle this was a heavy load. She once reluctantly confessed that her husband's sin was buying books when, with six boys, she would have liked a refrigerator that worked.

Ada Tozer, farm born and nurtured, raised a large garden behind the house. Under her care it produced an abundance of fresh vegetables for the family table and pantry. She was also an expert seamstress. She made most of her own clothes as well as Becky's. And besides these and other household activities, she found time to take the boys to the zoo, on picnics and other activities. At night, after the boys were put to bed, Ada played the piano and sang in her strong alto voice. She also maintained an extensive correspondence with Alliance missionaries and prayed regularly for them. All of this, Tozer, like many busy husbands, tended to take for granted.

There were times when Ada felt the strain and grew

a little impatient with her active husband. His very popularity as a speaker and writer added to her frustration. He was at times absentminded to her needs and feelings, yet in spite of this, they maintained a generally happy marriage. Had it not been for her dedication to the home, he could not have been as successful in his calling.

As the boys married, Ada mellowed appreciably. Her daughters-in-law were women she could relate to and talk with. She found satisfaction in these contacts and welcomed them.

Christmas was always a special time in the Tozer household. It was the one time of the year that Tozer was home with his family for any length of time. Although there was never an abundance of money, the parents succeeded in making it special for the children.

Especially after the boys married, Christmas generated plenty of activity and anticipation for Ada Tozer. As her sons arrived with their wives and children, the household census could swell to 20 or 30. The daughters-in-law pitched in, giving Ada a hand with the huge Christmas dinner. Mrs. Tozer always looked forward to Christmas and these family visits.

Circle of friends

Tozer's circle of friends was intentionally small. He was a very private man: some said a recluse, but that was not true. It was just that Tozer was very careful with his friendships. He never, for example, would let any of the inner circle know just how much they really meant to him. For Tozer, friendships were one of the things he believed he had to give up in order to wholly follow the Lord. People could never get to the core of Tozer because the core was elsewhere—in God Himself.

"You must be willing to give up your friends," Tozer would often say, "if you want to have the Friend." Friends and God were incompatible, in Tozer's thinking, and he never permitted anything to come between him and his Lord. He forsook all—literally—to follow Jesus.

Even at church, Tozer avoided people. He said he did not care to have people with "diseased personalities" coming up to shake his hand. He habitually entered the service while the congregation was singing the first hymn. After pronouncing the benediction, instead of greeting worshipers, he retreated to his study until most of the people had left.

Ada Tozer, with a decidedly different attitude toward people, saw to it that the Tozer household was hospitable—at least on Sundays. She even involved her preacher-husband in the task. Ada was a good meat-and-potatoes cook, and almost every Sunday she prepared a large feast. During the Sunday morning service, she would compile a tentative guest list. Anyone who looked lonely was subject to her invitation. By the time Sunday dinner was ready, there would be from 10 to 20 people around the table.

Tozer, spent from his morning's activities, did little to help get things ready, but after dinner he took charge of the dirty dishes. Enlisting a couple of his boys, he would wash the dishes while they wiped and put them away.

It was never quite clear whether Tozer acted altruistically or simply to escape the Sunday crowd in his living room. By the time the dishwashing was done, the dinner guests usually were gone.

TOZER-GRAMS

When God sets out to really make a superior Christian, He is compelled to strip the man of everything that might serve as a false refuge, a secondary trust. He must shut the man up to Himself only, or He must give him up to be a second-rate saint.

One of the greatest hindrances to spiritual poise and balanced living is the tendency to accept as correct images seen out of focus. What looks to a tired eye like a strange monster walking across the brow of a distant hill may be in reality only a beetle walking across the windowpane close at hand (as every reader of Poe will remember).

Harmful or vain speech blocks revival and grieves the Spirit more than we are likely to realize. It destroys the accumulative effect of spiritual impressions and makes it necessary each Sunday to recapture the devotional mood which has been lost during the week. Thus we are compelled constantly to do over again the work of last week and to retake ground lost by unprofitable conversation.

PRAYER

O God, be Thou exalted over my possessions. Nothing of earth's treasures shall seem dear unto me if only Thou art glorified in my life. Be Thou exalted over my friendships. I am determined that Thou shalt be above all, though I must stand deserted and alone in the midst of the earth. Be Thou exalted above my comforts. Though it mean the loss of bodily comforts and the carrying of heavy crosses I shall keep my vow made this day before Thee. Be Thou exalted over my reputation. Make me ambitious to please Thee even if as a result I must sink into obscurity and my name be forgotten as a dream. Rise, O Lord, into Thy proper place of honor, above my ambitions, above my likes and dislikes, above my family, my health and even life itself. Let me decrease that Thou mayest increase, let me sink that Thou mayest rise above. Ride forth upon me as Thou didst ride into Jerusalem mounted upon the humble little beast, a colt, the foal of an ass, and let me hear the children cry to Thee, "Hosanna in the highest."

"Restoring the Creator-Creature Relation"
The Pursuit of God

PERSONAL GLIMPSES

Council

At the 1959 Council in Buffalo, New York, I saw Dr. Tozer sitting in the lobby of the hotel, so as a young pastor I introduced myself and asked for some pointers on how to get along with church boards. His advice: "Never let your church board go up and down your back with a spiritual screwdriver, because they will try to adjust you. I used to walk into the pulpit lopsided because of all the adjustments."

Leonard Blight

Some of my best memories of Tozer were during the business sessions of General Council. He was a formidable foe in a debate. I cannot think of a single time when his position did not settle the vote of Council and bring the matter to a conclusion. He generally wrote out an outline of his debate and would stand, swaying in something of a circular form, and go through his entire debate with the greatest of oratorical skill. He left no stone unturned. He was not always kind. The only time I ever saw him really sarcastic was in the course of a debate on the Council floor and he had a real skill for that.

Perhaps the most devastating occurrence was the time he debated the National Association of Evangelicals' issue at the Council of 1946. A motion had been made that the Alliance join the organization. Tozer stood to his feet and killed the issue in a matter of minutes and it was never reviewed until after his death.

One of his pet peeves was long, drawn out debates at Council. One of my most vivid memories of A.W. Tozer was at the Winnipeg Council when the subject of the debate was the establishment of an Office of Education at headquarters and the employment of a Director of Education.

The debate lasted well into the afternoon of the closing day of Council. Everyone was weary and ready to leave. I had gone out of the auditorium, and A.W. Tozer came down the side of the building shaking his head. As he approached me, he said, "Every year I go home from this Council and fast and pray and say to God that I will never attend another one." Of course he was there in his usual place at the very next Council.

Dr. Keith M. Bailey

He was loyal in spirit to the fellowship of The Christian and Missionary Alliance where he served all of his life, but his heart and ministry were too lofty, too majestic to be bound by any denominational line. He belonged to the true church of God universal.

William F. Bryan

"Like many others, I consider his book *The Knowledge of the Holy* to be a devotional classic. I return to it frequently and have the feeling he is standing not far off, urging and encouraging me to think more highly of the God I serve."

Dr. David Rambo
President, The Christian and
Missionary Alliance

16

Potpourri

Tozer refused to wear a theological label. When he candidated in Chicago, he was interviewed by the church's official board. One board member—a good and spiritual man—was very sensitive about doctrine.

"Brother," he said, addressing the 31-year-old pastoral candidate, "what is your doctrine?"

Tozer was not the least bit intimidated by the question. "I am an ordained minister in The Christian and Missionary Alliance," he replied. And that ended the discussion.

"It may be a good thing I never went to seminary," Tozer used to say. "As God's hungry bee, I'm able to suck nectar out of all sorts of flowers." For example, he carried on a correspondence for some time with Thomas Merton, a Trappist monk.

Labels did not mean much to Tozer. The direction a person was facing was all that mattered. He said, "I refuse to allow any man to put his glasses on me and force me to see everything in his light. I love all God's children."

Tozer prefaced the final sermon in a series of messages based on John 17 by remarking, "I would like to announce that I have just preached myself into eternal security!" On another occasion, when he was preaching from the text, "Demas, because he loved this world, has deserted me" (2 Timothy 4:10), Tozer took a much less certain stand. "Some of my friends," he said, "would have Demas in heaven playing a harp with the saints. Other of my friends would have him at the opposite extremity. Personally, I don't know. All I can say is that the last time we see Demas he was walking in the wrong direction." And that is where Tozer left the matter.

"I go along with Graham Scroggie," he told one interrogator. "When someone asked Scroggie if he was a Calvinist or an Arminian, he answered, 'I am a Calvinist when I pray and an Arminian when I preach.' "

Raymond McAfee worked with Dr. Tozer closer and longer than anyone else. McAfee's outlook on ministry was similar to Tozer's and at the same time was greatly molded by Tozer. McAfee was a student at Wheaton and an announcer at a local Christian radio station when a friend told him that the Southside Alliance Church was looking for a choir director. McAfee immediately made an appointment to see about the position. Years later McAfee recalled that first meeting.

"I remember my first experience with him. I went down to have an interview about becoming choir director and I attended his Sunday school class. He had a large men's class that he taught in the upper room of the old building. He was teaching on Colossians 3:4, 'Put off therefore.' During his teaching he made this remark. 'There's Mrs. Deitz [of Dietz Publishing, later merged with Christian Publications], God bless her memory. You wouldn't anymore expect to find Mrs. Deitz doing these things than you would expect to find archangels shooting craps.' And I tell you," McAfee continued, "we all perished. Afterwards I talked with him for a while. I knew that he was a well-known preacher and that he had had some tremendous choir directors, and I was nervous. I didn't know what to expect, but he was cordial and to the point. He took me to the choir library and showed me the library and asked me if I knew this and did I know that. I told him that I could learn the ones I didn't know. Well, he accepted me on a month's probation." This started a relationship that was to last until Tozer's death.

Married to his sweaters

Those who knew Tozer personally and worked with him in Chicago knew that he was married to his sweaters because he was always cold. McAfee accused Tozer of trying to take care of the two blood corpuscles that chased each other around through his system.

"I think I have you figured out," McAfee once said to Tozer. "You take your sweater off the 31st of July and put it back on the 1st of August." Thinking for a moment, Tozer replied, "Yes, I think you're right."

One day when McAfee came into Tozer's study, Tozer said, "McAfee, do you know what? I took a bath last night and what do you think I found?"

"I don't know, Dr. Tozer," McAfee responded, thinking that he had discovered something dreadfully wrong with himself. "What did you find?"

With mock seriousness Tozer explained. "Last night I took a bath and found a sweater that I forgot I put on."

Tozer's home was some five miles from the Chicago church and each day he rode the bus to his church office. He would come dressed in a suit and tie, but immediately upon arriving at the church office he would take off his trousers and put on a pair of what he called his "praying pants." There was no permanent press in those days and to preserve the crease in his trousers he would don these other pants.

The back seam of the "praying pants" was slit down some considerable distance, so McAfee once asked him, "Dr. Tozer, how do you know how to put those pants on?"

"Oh that's easy, Ray," Dr. Tozer responded. "The back pockets go this way."

Off to the side of Tozer's office was a washroom.

One day McAfee went in to wash his hands. In the washroom was a towel that belonged to Tozer's son, Forrest, a marine who had been wounded in the Korean war. The towel was a drab olive gray. McAfee said to Tozer, "Why don't you wash this towel?"

"McAfee," Tozer replied, "20 people have dried their hands on that towel and you're the first to complain."

Tozer's love of children was legendary. One day he and McAfee left the church for lunch at a nearby restaurant. Just down the street they happened upon a grimy little boy playing on the sidewalk. Tozer stopped.

"How old are you, sonny?"

Without looking up, the little fellow answered, "I'm three."

"You couldn't possibly be three years old," Tozer objected.

His integrity assailed, the boy at last looked up. "I am, too," he asserted. "I am three years old!"

"No," insisted Tozer. "You couldn't possibly be three. Nobody could get that dirty in three years!"

Use of humor

Tozer had an irrepressible humor, which he strived to control, though not always successfully. When physically tired, his guard tended to slip. McAfee used to say, "I could always tell how tired he was by the amount of humor that sneaked into his sermons. If the congregation was convulsed with laughter, Tozer was tired."

Once Tozer was scheduled to preach for a week in Buffalo, New York, starting Monday evening. He arrived in Buffalo late Monday afternoon, tired from his Sunday ministry and the long train trip. Louis L. King, who later would gain distinction as president of The Christian and Missionary Alliance, was at the time a pastor in the area. King brought a Presbyterian woman to the Monday night service who had read Tozer's writings and was anxious to hear the man in person.

"Never before or since have I seen Tozer quite as humorous as he was that night," King remembers. "From start to finish, his address was so uncontrollably humorous that my Presbyterian guest, who had false teeth, had to use a hymnbook to keep her teeth in her mouth."

Tozer was being introduced as the keynote speaker at an Alliance General Council. "When I learned that I would be introducing Dr. Tozer tonight," the meeting chairman began, "I sought advice on how to do it. Someone informed me that if I didn't do it right, I would hear about it before he preached. So I went to Dr. Tozer and asked him how he wanted to be introduced. In accordance with his wishes, let me just say, Dr. Tozer will now preach."

Tozer ambled to the podium amid the wave of laughter that followed the chairman's brief introduction. He stood there, dead pan, until all was quiet. "If the good brother remembers," Tozer began, "I said to say, 'Brother Tozer will now preach.' "

When some of Chicago's more liberal churches invited evangelist Billy Graham to the city for a crusade, the city's fundamentalist preachers called a meeting to decide what their stance should be. Tozer, by then a well-known figure among fundamentalists, attended.

The debate was long. Tozer had taken a seat along the wall. From time to time he jotted down notes. Finally, he stood up and asked to speak.

"Yes, Dr. Tozer," the chairman responded. "We all want to hear what you have to say on this matter."

"Mr. Chairman," Tozer began, his voice so low that people had to strain to hear him. "I want to say that I have met Billy Graham. He did me the great honor of coming to see me in my study. I don't agree with everything Billy Graham says any more than I agree with everything anybody else says. But I want to warn you about something. It is possible for any of us to run against the wrong object and bend our lance for good."

Tozer paused a moment to let that observation sink in. "Now, come on brethren," he continued, "let's let our hair down. You could stand all the fundamentalists in the United States in one line and start them preaching, and they would have less effect on the United States than Billy Graham would have just clearing his throat."

Billy Graham got the cooperation of most of Greater Chicago's conservative churches.

Friendship with R.R. Brown

One person that Dr. Tozer enjoyed was Dr. Robert R. Brown, of Omaha, Nebraska. Dr. Brown founded the Preacher's Chorus, a feature for many years at

General Council of The Christian and Missionary Alliance. Tozer would sometimes sneak into the choir practice sessions just to have Brown throw him out.

"Tozer," Brown would yell when he saw Tozer in the choir. "What are you doing here? Get out of my choir. I won't have it!"

With a big grin on his face, Tozer would slowly walk out. He loved it, and so did Dr. Brown.

On the General Council floor, Brown always had something to say and nobody could say it quite like him. During one Council session Brown had made a florid speech, as all his speeches were. During a break in the business session for lunch, Tozer and McAfee were walking through the lobby when Tozer saw Brown with a crowd of young preachers around him. "Come on, McAfee," Tozer said. "I want to talk to Brown." Across the lobby he went to where Brown was.

"Brown," Tozer said, "I want to ask you a question if you'll promise not to get mad. Now you promise you won't get mad when I ask this?"

"Yes, yes, Tozer," Brown said impatiently. "What's your question?"

"Well, Brown," Tozer slowly began, "I just wanted to ask you, what side of the issue are you on? I couldn't tell from your speech in there." With a twinkle in his eye he quickly added. "Look, Brown, you promised not to get mad." Before Dr. Brown could get in a word Tozer walked off chuckling with his hand over his mouth, bouncing his shoulders, not making much noise but enjoying putting one over on Brown. They were good friends and had utmost respect for each other. No two people could have been more opposite than A.W. Tozer and R.R. Brown. They were pleasantly critical of each other and both could take it as well as hand it out.

Another occasion when Tozer was being introduced, the person went on and on about the marvelous qualifications of the speaker for the evening. Finally, when Tozer got to the pulpit, his first remarks were, "All I can say is, dear God forgive him for what he said, and forgive me for enjoying it so much."

Incurable tease

Tozer was an incurable tease, and if he ever got anything on you, woe be you. He never forgot it, and in the most unexpected moment he would bring it up.

Once he approached two young women in the Chicago church; one was new to the church while the other had grown up in it.

"Do you know the difference," Tozer asked the new girl, "between a vision and a sight?"

"No, Dr. Tozer," she replied quite seriously, "I can't say that I do."

"Well," he said, "You're a vision, she's a sight." With that he walked off chuckling to himself, never waiting for a response.

Once Tozer became ill and his family forced him to go to a doctor for a checkup. The doctor diagnosed his problem as appendicitis and tried to convince him that his appendix needed to come out. Tozer adamantly refused.

"Doctor, why are you always trying to get a butcher

knife in me? I'm not going to let you take anything out!" And he did not.

Years later, Tozer and the doctor happened to meet. After they had greeted each other, Tozer brought up the subject of his appendix.

"What about this, doctor?" Tozer asked. "Years ago you said I had to have my appendix removed. I never did, and I feel great!"

"Oh," the doctor grunted in disgust, "your appendix dried up and blew away a long time ago!"

Tozer was a thinker. It might take time, but Tozer insisted on doing his own thinking, arriving at his own conclusions. Once while Ira Gerig was director of music at Southside Alliance, Tozer emerged from his study, sauntered over to the piano where Gerig was working, and sat down beside him on the bench.

"Gerig," Tozer complained, "I must be going soft in the head. I haven't had one original thought all week."

Not a visiting pastor

Tozer's reputation for not visiting the members of his parish was widely known. He felt he could not devote necessary time to visitation and still be the pulpit minister his congregation expected him to be. That matter he had settled with the church board before he accepted its call. So he limited his visits to the critically ill among the church's membership. One story quickly made the rounds and by now has achieved legend status.

Tozer had flown in from an out-of-city speaking mission, and in the course of the drive from airport to home, the member who had met him remarked that so-and-so, a church elder, was in the hospital recovering from minor surgery. Since their route would take them right by the hospital, Tozer suggested that they stop and visit the man.

When the elder saw Tozer enter his room, he blanched. "Surely, I'm not that sick, am I?" he exclaimed in alarm. Turning to his wife, also in the room, he asked, "Are you sure the doctors told me everything?"

Years later Tozer tried to deny the story, but then weakly admitted, "It could have happened."

TOZER-GRAMS

Every ransomed man owes his salvation to the fact that during the days of his sinning God kept the door of mercy open by refusing to accept any of his evil acts as final.

The lone hope for a sinning man is that for a while God will not accept his sinful conduct as decisive. He will hold judgment in suspension, giving the sinner opportunity either to reverse himself by repentance or to commit the final act that will close the books against him forever.

It is a none too subtle form of egotism to picture ourselves as great sinners, letting our imagination mount till we see ourselves strong and dangerous rebels, after the likeness of Milton's Satan, actually threatening the security of the throne of God. We thus dramatize ourselves to hide our pitiful weakness.

That a man, by his sin, may ruin himself and greatly injure others is true. His sin, when seen in relation to himself and others is great; but when set over against the boundless power and limitless resources of Deity, it is nothing at all.

In baseball a man will sometimes "play over his own head," which is to say that he will, for a brief time, rise above his average ability as a day by day player. No manager would sign a man on such an erratic performance. He wants to know what the player is capable of doing game after game against all kinds of opposition.

PRAYER

Teach us, O God, that nothing is necessary to Thee. Were anything necessary to Thee that thing would be the measure of Thine imperfection: and how could we worship one who is imperfect? If nothing is necessary to Thee, then no one is necessary, and if no one, then not we. Thou dost seek us though Thou dost not need us. We seek Thee because we need Thee, for in Thee we live and move and have our being. Amen.

"The Self-sufficiency of God"
The Knowledge of the Holy

"If a sermon can be compared to light, then A.W. Tozer released a laser beam from the pulpit, a beam that penetrated your heart, seared your conscience, exposed sin, and left you crying, 'What must I do to be saved?' The answer was always the same: surrender to Christ; get to know God personally; grow to become like Him."

Warren W. Wiersbe
The Best of A.W. Tozer

17

Toronto

Tozer was facing possibly the hardest decision he had been called on to make. For more than three decades Southside Alliance in Chicago had been the focus of his labor and ministry. Southside Alliance was home. It was the place where he felt the most comfortable.

But these were the late 1950s. For several years civil and racial unrest had been accelerating in Chicago. The neighborhood around the church had deteriorated irreparably. Many members were afraid to attend services, especially on Sunday evenings. A large segment of the congregation had already moved into the suburbs. Southside Alliance was one of the few major churches that had not yet followed its members into the calmer suburban environs. The church board was of a mind to make the flight from the inner city unanimous.

Tozer agreed with the board that relocation was the only solution. But he did not agree that he should lead such a migration. He had been through one building program 22 years earlier; at age 62 he did not relish the responsibility of another. This move would demand a different kind of ministry than the one God had given him.

Twenty-five years later a substantial church faced with a similar problem would simply add an administrator to its staff. In the late '50s in The Christian and Missionary Alliance, one pastor was expected to do everything. In Tozer's thinking that one pastor should be a younger man with spiritual gifts other than the ones he possessed.

A year earlier, convinced of these realities, Tozer had tendered his resignation to the church board. With ardent emotion the board had refused to accept it. But the ensuing year had only confirmed to him the need for a change.

Still, after 31 years of ministry in the same church, it would be hard to walk away. Gazing about the small church study, Tozer eyed the familiar contents of the room: the shelves lined with books—books he had personally sought and acquired, books that had become good friends, guiding him in his quest for God, books that were gentle mementos of his pilgrimage toward spiritual reality.

The sofa over in the corner was the scene of many spiritual struggles and victories as he knelt beside it in solitary hours of prayer and worship. There was no way to measure the blessings that had come to him in this inner sanctuary where he was alone with God. The room held an abundance of sacred memories. God had been so near. Here he had discovered so much about God.

If Chicago was a different city from the one that greeted Tozer in 1928, the pastor of Southside Alliance had also changed. When Tozer arrived in Chicago, he was 31 years old and little known. Now he had a worldwide reputation. D. Martin Lloyd-Jones, the celebrated London pulpiteer, for years had tried to get Tozer to go to England for a preaching mission. Tozer's *Alliance Life* editorials were simultaneously printed in England's *Life of Faith* paper. His books had been translated into many languages and were selling well. He was known and respected in the evangelical community as both a spokesman and a prophet to his generation.

Faced with a decision

When faced with a decision, Tozer's style was to confer only with God and seek His mind. The answer might take a few days or even several years, but Tozer was determined to know the mind of God on the situation at issue. In his study that morning, his thoughts raced back over the years, the events, the people. This very church building, for example, with its many wonderful memories—could it all be coming to an end? Was it really time for him to move?

And where would he go? It was hard to think of any place other than Chicago. For several years Tozer had been thinking of withdrawing from pastoral ministry to devote more time to *Alliance Life* and the many Bible conferences to which he was invited to speak. Perhaps this was the time to do just that—after 40 years of pastoral ministry. Maybe God would free him from the pastorate.

As he reflected and prayed, the course became clear—or at least the first step became clear. He framed it in a letter to the church board dated June 27, 1959.

"After more than 30 years of serving the Chief Shepherd, Jesus Christ our Lord, as undershepherd of this flock, the time appears to be drawing near when I must relinquish my very pleasant duties and withdraw from this church. I therefore tender my resignation."

He told the board his reasons were "mainly two." One, he felt compelled to finish "certain spiritual labors," which he could not do while simultaneously pastoring a church. Two, the relocation of the church demanded "a different kind of minister" if the church was to succeed.

The board, realizing that Tozer's convictions were "too deep and too conclusive" to be countered, accepted his resignation with the utmost reluctance. But it left the door open should Tozer have second thoughts.

When news of Tozer's resignation broke, all sorts of

churches tried to entice him to their pulpits. Tozer turned a deaf ear to them all. He believed the time had come for him to concentrate on his writing and on conference preaching. At the time, the headquarters of The Christian and Missionary Alliance, including the main *Alliance Life* offices, was in New York City. Tozer intended to locate in the metropolitan New York area to be close to Alliance headquarters.

One perception he went out of his way to squelch: He was not retiring. At his resignation, he told his Chicago congregation, "I'll preach as long as I can hold a Bible." Alluding to Israel's priests, he observed that they "began their ministry when they were 30 and finished it when they were 50." Thus they had only 20 years of active ministry.

"But," Tozer added, "prophets never retired, so I'm not retiring, except to put on new tires to go a little faster and farther."

Avenue Road persisted

Of all the churches that invited Tozer to be their pastor, there was one that refused to take no for an answer. Avenue Road Church in Toronto would not give up that easily. Avenue Road was a large church in downtown Toronto that had recently aligned itself with The Christian and Missionary Alliance. Only The People's Church, founded—and still at that time led—by Oswald J. Smith was larger.

When Tozer turned down the invitation of Avenue Road Church, the board appealed immediately to the district superintendent, William J. Newell. "What will it take," they wanted to know, "to get Dr. Tozer here as our pastor?" Together they discussed what they would expect of Tozer if he were to agree to come to Toronto. Finally the superintendent brought the meeting to a close. "I believe I know how to get your candidate here. Pray for me; I am going to give him a telephone call."

Mr. Newell's request was an innocuous one. Would Dr. Tozer be willing to fill the pulpit at Avenue Road Church one Sunday?

"I'll go anywhere to preach," Tozer responded, and the two men settled on a Sunday. "But," Tozer cautioned, "it needs to be clear that I am not interested in being the pastor of Avenue Road Church."

The Sunday arrived. When Tozer got up to preach, his first remark was, "I want you to understand that I am not a pastoral candidate." The audience took his remark good-naturedly. Tozer preached morning and evening. The sanctuary was filled for both services, with a large number of college and university students among those in attendance. There was a good response to Tozer's sermons.

After the evening service, Superintendent Newell requested Tozer to meet with the church board.

"What about it?" Newell asked, turning to Tozer after the meeting had convened. "You've refused the church's invitation to be its pastor, but would you be willing simply to preach here twice each Sunday? We have a young man who will be taking the pastorate. He will handle everything. You won't have to attend board meetings, visit the sick, lay any cornerstones, attend any picnics, cut any ribbons or anything else. Just preach twice a Sunday, that's all. After that, *Alliance Life* can have you."

The proposal took Tozer aback. He had not anticipated an offer like that. He would have to give it thought. On the surface, it seemed too good to refuse.

"Well," he said finally, "if you'll stick to your bargain and won't expect any more of me and will turn me loose to write and edit the magazine and won't bother me, won't get in my way or tell me what I ought to preach—well, maybe I'll consider it."

One small step. The board members were delighted. They set the whole church to praying.

And Tozer set himself once more to decision-making. Toronto seemed ripe for a pulpit ministry such as he could have in the city. He was particularly interested in the many universities and colleges. He had worked cooperatively with Inter-Varsity Christian Fellowship for many years, and there was a large, active chapter at the University of Toronto.

On the other hand, the evangelical voices in the city were remarkably few. Oswald J. Smith stood head and shoulders above any others, but he was out of town more often than not. People rarely got to hear him preach. Avenue Road Church had a long reputation as a center-city church with an evangelical, deeper life ministry.

By midweek, Tozer had made his decision. He called Avenue Road Church to accept the invitation to be the preaching pastor—but only for a few months. Tozer still planned to move to New York City to be near the *Alliance Life* offices.

Those "few months" turned into almost four years. His ministry in Toronto was some of the richest he had ever enjoyed. The church responded enthusiastically. The large sanctuary was filled for almost every service. His conference ministry increased as well. Beyond the midpoint of his sixth decade, Tozer evidenced no slowing down, no decrease in the quality of his sermons.

The transplant operation had been successful after all!

TOZER-GRAMS

When I say that a church is dead, I do not mean only that its members are apathetic and slow to respond to the promptings of the Spirit. I mean something more terrible than that; I mean that its words and deeds have not the Spirit of life in them.

The knowledge of God is the most glorious treasure anyone could possess, yet in most civilized countries there is but one institution engaged in promoting that knowledge, and even that institution is not working very hard at it.

There is a glorious catholicity of the saints, a mystic brotherhood of the farsighted who have long been straining their eyes to catch a glimpse of the King in His beauty in the land that is very far off. With great joy and deep humility I claim membership in that brotherhood. This is the oldest and largest church in the world; it is the church of the cross-smitten, of the God-enamored.

The spiritual giants of old would not take their religion the easy way nor offer to God that which cost them nothing. They sought not comfort by holiness, and the pages of history are still wet with their blood and their tears.

We now live in softer times. Woe unto us, for we have become adept in the art of comforting ourselves with power.

PRAYER

Our Father, we know that Thou art present with us, but our knowledge is but a figure and shadow of truth and has little of the spiritual savor and inward sweetness such knowledge should afford. This is for us a great loss and the cause of much weakness of heart. Help us to make at once such amendment of life as is necessary before we can experience the true meaning of the words "In Thy presence is fulness of joy." Amen.

"God's Omnipresence"
The Knowledge of the Holy

PERSONAL GLIMPSES

Effective Ministry

In 1979 I had occasion to be in England for a month. In Nottingham I met some Chinese students who were studying there in England. When we were having dinner over at their house, one of the girls brought a book to me and said, "Do you know this person?" It happened to be *That Incredible Christian*, which I had compiled and for which I had written the foreword. When I turned to that page and showed them that I had written the foreword, I can tell you they had a great deal more respect for me!

Anita Bailey

It was eight months after coming under the ministry of Dr. Tozer that I moved away, and I thought I was kind of glad to get away because things were getting pretty hot for me. But I had heard enough so that even though I was away from Chicago I came to know Christ all by myself up in my bedroom out on a farm. Then I couldn't wait to get back and tell the people how Christ had come into my life. I never wanted to miss a service. Even as a young believer I always seemed to be going to the altar because something in his message hit me right where I was living.

Esther King

"I had the privilege of conversing with Dr. Tozer on matters relative to revival in our time. He then expressed the longing that he might live to see the day when God would 'rend the heavens, and . . . come down' in showers of blessing. . . . If ever there was a man in our generation who could hasten the day of revival it was Dr. A.W. Tozer. Although I knew him only a few years, he deeply impressed me as a man of outstanding spiritual qualities. He certainly had a knowledge of the Holy, and a few minutes in his presence made it evident that he walked with God. He was a respected leader within The Christian and Missionary Alliance and a penetrating writer of unusual depth and breadth, an evangelical voice of authority and clarity to the church at large and an uncompromising preacher of righteousness."

Stephen F. Olford

18

The Goal

Several years after Tozer left his ministry in Chicago, the congregation invited him back for the dedication of their new building. The church had purchased land about five miles from their old site and erected a beautiful new sanctuary. It was Tozer's honor to preach the dedication sermon.

Members of the Chicago church had been sending Tozer pictures of the building in its various phases of construction. To see it in its finished form was a moving experience for him. "I'm sorry I didn't stay until I saw the congregation over into this new building," Tozer remarked to J. Francis Chase. "It is more beautiful than I expected it to be."

Writing and preaching

The years in Toronto went quickly. In addition to his pulpit and magazine ministries, he completed work on his landmark book *The Knowledge of the Holy*, a study of the attributes of God. Some consider it his finest piece of work. He also completed *The Christian Book of Mystical Verse*, a compilation of the writings of many of the saints Tozer delighted in. He looked forward to writing one more book—on worship. The theme was the subject of some of the last sermons he preached in Toronto. Nearly 25 years after his death, Christian Publications issued the book posthumously. Entitled *Whatever Happened to Worship?*, it is based on his sermon series, tape-recorded by the church.

In the summer of 1962, he returned briefly to Chicago for the denominational Life Investment Conference. There he met at 6:30 each morning to preach to 1,200 youth from across North America.

That year Tozer also received an invitation to address the National Association of Evangelicals at their 1963 gathering. For reasons of his own, Tozer had little sympathy for this association. In 1946—not long after the founding of the N.A.E.—when The Christian and Missionary Alliance was considering joining the organization, Tozer in a caustic speech succeeded in defeating the proposal. Not until after his death 17 years later did the Alliance reconsider and join.

"Are you just trying to butter me up," Tozer wanted to know, "or do you think I really have something to say?" Reassured that the invitation was genuine, he went and preached to the organization.

In May, 1963, Tozer experienced some chest pain. Except for the mild heart attack earlier in his Chicago pastorate that kept him from the pulpit for several months, he had enjoyed generally good health throughout life despite the pace he set for himself. These chest pains were probably not threatening, but he was 66.

His condition improved quickly and he looked forward to being discharged Sunday, May 12. The date was critical. The Alliance General Council would convene Wednesday, the 15th, and he was scheduled to be the Sunday evening speaker, May 19th. For many years Tozer had preached the Sunday evening sermon at General Council. The delegates looked forward to those sermons, and Tozer always seemed to be at his best when he was preaching to his "brethren."

When Ada arrived at the hospital Saturday evening to visit her husband, he reminded her that she should pick him up early the next morning. That would allow ample travel time to reach Phoenix, Arizona, where Council would convene that year.

During the visit, one of the hospital nurses brought a baby into the room. She knew Tozer's fondness for babies, and she let Tozer hold the baby a few minutes. At 10 o'clock Ada kissed her husband good night and set out for home. Tozer was soon asleep.

An hour later a nurse went in to check on Tozer and discovered that he was in the midst of a coronary thrombosis—a heart attack. Staff efforts to stabilize his condition were not successful. Shortly after midnight, on Sunday, May 12, 1963, not quite a week after preaching his last sermon, Aiden Wilson Tozer found himself "away from the body and at home with the Lord."

Memorial services were held both in Toronto and in Chicago. His body was laid to rest in a small cemetery in Ellat, a section of Akron, Ohio. A simple epitaph is inscribed on his stone: A Man of God.

At the funeral, his daughter Becky made a comment that was typical of something her father himself might have said. "I can't feel sad," she remarked. "I know Dad's happy. He has lived for this all his life."

One of Tozer's sons later commented on his father, "He burned himself out for Christ. That's the way he wanted to go. He knew the end was coming and he talked about it matter-of-factly. He was ready. He knew that Christ was in him, and what happened to him was up to God."

Francis Chase, one of Tozer's few close friends, was asked to participate in the Chicago memorial service.

"Dr. Tozer," he said, "often remarked in his matchless manner when speaking of a Christian who had departed this life, 'Well, by God's grace and goodness, he made it.' Yea, and amen, good brother, you 'made it,' too. Farewell for a little while."

The pursuit was over. Tozer had reached his goal.

TOZER-GRAMS

Perpetual disciples are a reproach to any teacher. We should teach men and women how to walk alone, looking only to God for support. The quicker they can get along without us, the better we have done our job as teachers. The temptation to make ourselves indispensable is very strong, but we must learn to enjoy the pain of seeing our disciples catch up with us or even pass us on the way.

If we could only rise above our prejudices, we should see that all God's children bear a family resemblance to each other. And we should see also that no matter how loudly a man may protest his faith in Christ, no matter how often he may be found before the altar, if he has not the sign of the cross in his heart, he is for all his religion a man most miserable, a soul lost in the night.

The depths of a man's spirituality may be known quite accurately by the quality of his public prayers.

To get to the truth I recommend a plain text Bible and the diligent application of two knees to the

floor. Beware of too many footnotes. The rabbis of Israel took to appending notes to the inspired text, with the result that a great body of doctrine grew up which finally crowded out the Scriptures themselves.

I have on a few occasions been roasted to a rich brown over some personal idiosyncrasy which could not possibly do any harm, while the big weaknesses that really gave me trouble were either ignored altogether or made to pass for virtues!

PRAYER

O Majesty unspeakable, my soul desires to behold Thee. I cry to Thee from the dust.

Yet when I inquire after Thy name it is secret. Thou art hidden in the light which no man can approach unto. What Thou art cannot be thought or uttered, for Thy glory is ineffable.

Still, prophet and psalmist, apostle and saint have encouraged me to believe that I may in some measure know Thee. Therefore, I pray, whatever of Thyself Thou hast been pleased to disclose, help me to search out as treasure more precious than rubies or the merchandise of fine gold: for with Thee shall I live when the stars of the twilight are no more and the heavens have vanished away and only Thou remainest. Amen.

"A Divine Attribute:
Something True About God"
The Knowledge of the Holy

Appendix

A.W. Tozer recommended these books for those who would know "the deep things of God." In making his recommendations, Dr. Tozer did not uncritically approve the entire contents of these writings. Rather, he offered the list as the products of men and women who ardently loved their Lord. Any doctrinal defects in the books would be far outbalanced by their spiritual verities.

The Adornment of the Spiritual Marriage . . . . Jan van Ruysbroeck
Amendment of Life . . . . Richard Rolle
The Ascent of Mt. Carmel . . . . John of the Cross
The Ascent of Mt. Zion . . . . . . Berdardeno de Laredo
The Book of Eternal Wisdom . . . . .Heinrich Suso
Centuries of Meditations . . . . .Thomas Traherne
Christian Perfection . . . . Francois Fenelon
The Cloud of Unknowing . . . . Anonymous
Confessions . . . . St. Augustine
The Dark Night of the Soul . . . . John of the Cross

The Goad of Love .... Walter Hilton
A Guide to True Peace
.... Miguel de Molinos and others
Hymns .... Gerhard Tersteegen
The Imitation of Christ .... Thomas a Kempis
Introduction to a Devout Life .... De Sales
Letters of Direction .... de Tourville
On the Incarnation .... Athanasius
On the Love of God .... Bernard of Clairvaux
Poems .... Frederick Faber
Poems .... Isaac Watts
The Practice of the Presence of God . . Brother Lawrence
Private Devotions .... Lancelot Andrewes
Proslogion .... Anselm of Canterbury
The Quiet Way .... Gerhard Tersteegen
Sixteen Revelations of Divine Love
.... Juliana of Norwich
The Scale of Perfection .... Walter Hilton
Sermons .... Johannes Tauler
Song of Songs .... Bernard of Clairvaux
The Spiritual Combat .... Lorenzo Scupoli
Spiritual Guide .... Miguel de Molinos
Talks of Instruction .... Meister Eckhart
A Testament of Devotion .... Thomas Kelly
Theologia Germanica (Winkworth Translation)
.... Anonymous
The Vision of God .... Nicholas of Cusa
The Way of Christ .... Jakob Boehme

Available books by Dr. A.W. Tozer

A.W. Tozer: An Anthology
The Best of A.W. Tozer
Born after Midnight
Christ the Eternal Son
The Christian Book of Mystical Verse
The Divine Conquest
Echoes from Eden
Faith Beyond Reason
Gems from Tozer
God Tells the Man Who Cares
How to be Filled with the Holy Spirit
I Call It Heresy
I Talk Back to the Devil
Jesus, Author of Our Faith
Jesus Is Victor
Jesus, Our Man in Glory
Keys to the Deeper Life
The Knowledge of the Holy
Leaning into the Wind
Let My People Go: The Life of Robert A. Jaffray
Man: The Dwelling Place of God
Men Who Met God
The Next Chapter after the Last
Of God and Men
Paths to Power
The Price of Neglect
The Pursuit of God
Renewed Day by Day
Renewed Day by Day, Volume 2

The Root of the Righteous
The Set of the Sail
That Incredible Christian
This World: Playground or Battleground?
Tragedy in the Church: The Missing Gifts
A Treasury of A.W. Tozer
We Travel an Appointed Way
Whatever Happened to Worship?
When He Is Come
Who Put Jesus on the Cross?
Wingspread

Bibliography

Dr. A.W. Tozer Memorial Issue of *The Alliance Witness*, July 24, 1963.

Enlow, David. "Can Fundamentalism Be Saved?" *Christian Life,* August 1954.

_____. "Lessons From a 20th Century Prophet." *Moody Monthly*, September 1980.

Fant, David J., Jr. *A.W. Tozer: A Twentieth-Century Prophet.* Harrisburg, PA: Christian Publications, 1964.

Mains, Karen Burton. "Up from the Misty Lowlands." *Christian Herald*, November 1980.

Snyder, James L. "A Profile in Devotion." *Alliance Life*, May 11, 1988.

_____. "A.W. Tozer: A Man In Pursuit of God." *Fundamentalist Journal*, March 1986.

Tozer, A.W. *Keys to the Deeper Life.* Grand Rapids, MI: Zondervan Publishing House, 1984.

_____. *The Knowledge of the Holy.* San Francisco: Harper & Row, 1961.

_____. *The Pursuit of God.* Camp Hill, PA: Christian Publications, 1982.

Wiersbe, Warren. *The Best of A.W. Tozer.* Camp Hill, PA: Christian Publications, 1978.

_____. *Walking with the Giants.* Grand Rapids, MI: Baker Book House, 1976.

For additional copies of
In Pursuit of God
or information on the books by A.W. Tozer
contact your local Christian bookstore
or call Christian Publications, toll-free,
1-800-233-4443.